CW00881109

FUTURE
NEXT

JOHN SANEI &
IRAJ ABEDIAN

FUTURE
NEXT

RE-IMAGINING
OUR WORLD &
CONQUERING
UNCERTAINTY

JOHN SANEI &
IRAJ ABEDIAN

Published by Mercury
an imprint of Burnet Media

•

Burnet Media is the publisher of Mercury, Two Dogs and Two Pups books
info@burnetmedia.co.za
www.burnetmedia.co.za
PO Box 53557, Kenilworth, 7745,
South Africa

•

First published 2020

•

Text © 2020 Iraj Abedian, John Sanei
Cover image © Shutterstock

•

All rights reserved. No part of this publication may be reproduced, stored
in a retrieval system or transmitted, in any form or by any means,
electronic, mechanical, photocopying, recording or otherwise,
without the prior written permission of the copyright owners.

•

This POD edition printed, bound and distributed
by Amazon
www.amazon.com

•

Also available as an ebook

*To all those who have been angered
and awakened by Covid-19, and yet inspired
to mobilise in search of a new tomorrow
to avoid future human suffering.*

CONTENTS

PART III

PREFACE

This book is proof that nothing in our world is ever fixed or permanent – not even ideas captured in ink. Having begun life as two short ebooks released during lockdown in South Africa, *FutureNEXT* was always intended to evolve before publication in print form, but it has evolved more than I might have hoped or imagined.

The initial ebook, *FutureNOW*, was inspired by a dramatic leap in lifestyle and thought-space, when I went into lockdown on my family farm in Limpopo, South Africa, a continent away from my residence in Dubai. It was about coping with the immediate challenges of the Covid pandemic and resulting lockdowns.

The next leap of inspiration came while working on the second ebook, *FutureHOW*, when I realised I needed some heavyweight economic expertise on which to anchor my thoughts about ways to rethink the future. So I reached out to a hugely respected family friend, Dr Iraj Abedian, whose body of economic work with government, big business and at the IMF is world-leading. Critically, Iraj and I are both optimists at heart, who believe in the upward trajectory of human prosperity over time, and his willingness to come on board and combine our expertise in different fields left me particularly excited. It was an indicator that others, too, had recognised the opportunity for change that the pandemic has presented to us all.

Working closely with Iraj has been a privilege and a pleasure. It is a mark of his wisdom that, despite his authority and reputation, he remains so open-minded and willing to adapt to a world in Covid-catalysed transformation. But that is very much the point of *FutureNEXT*: encouraging a mindset ready to embrace necessary change.

Our intention was to create a guidebook for readers wondering how they might be part of this change. Together, we have reframed the original ebooks and added the critical third part that outlines our thinking for the path forward. We've done this in a way that I hope will help readers develop their own perspectives and philosophies, both as individuals and as members of our greater humanity, and will allow us all to accept what is happening around us and look through the chaos of today towards a better future.

John Sanei
September 2020

As the pandemic began sweeping the world in early 2020, and as I got used to working in a state of semi-lockdown, it became increasingly evident to me that humanity the world over is in the throes of an evolving and game-changing transformation. Covid-19 has proved the catalyst to an already existing evolution. And from it all, there seems to be a growing "mass wisdom" that the crisis is more of a symptom than a cause of some of humanity's major vulnerabilities.

As a student of economics, I have no doubt that beneath these open social conflicts lies an increasingly unfair socio-economic structure that has to be revolutionised and replaced by a new system that can facilitate a sustainable socio-economic life on planet Earth. This is not a new thought; humanity has made great strides since the Industrial Revolution of the late 1700s, but for many decades economists, statesmen and social scientists have been at pains to flag the need for a "new world order".

Now we appear to have reached a point where people everywhere are ready to heed and respond to the message. Such a transformation, I feel, has to be informed by the lessons of the past two centuries, empowered by the prevailing technology of our digital age and driven by the ever-changing structure of socio-economic and political power.

The good news is that I believe we now have the technology, tools, thinking and growing willingness to make it a reality. So when John approached me to work on a book together, I felt that the chance to promote this message was well worth taking. The ability and willingness for people to collaborate wherever we may be in the world is one of the profound powers of our time, where so much of our potential lies.

The idea of an ex-professor of economics-turned-public policy activist joining forces with a tech-minded futures thinker who speaks to audiences around the world might have been impossible not long ago. Today, I hope our book will serve as an introduction to an ongoing collective conversation, and perhaps play a small part in the necessary evolution of human society in the coming decades.

Iraj Abedian
September 2020

INTRODUCTION

So here we are in the future.

It's safe to say that it has arrived earlier than anybody expected.

Covid-19 has proven to be more than a mere disruptor: it has been an extreme accelerant that has heaved us further into the digital age and had us all scrambling for signs of certainty. And despite our desperation for things to return to "the way they were", the longer the pandemic remained a part of our lives, the clearer it became that this wouldn't happen. We won't be going back to the "normal" we knew.

But, as we maintain in the pages ahead, we shouldn't want to. The Covid pandemic has illustrated how old processes and economic foundations simply don't work the way they used to because they rest on levels of certainty that no longer exist. So we should rather use the opportunity the pandemic has presented us to find a new normal that's better than before.

The reason we may feel shaken by the realisation that we won't be returning to the familiarity of 2019 is because we are hardwired to seek out the safety of what we know. The battle our brains face between not being able to restart at our default setting, while simultaneously trying to plan ahead in an unknown world, has us feeling lost. We cannot anchor ourselves in what we know, and we cannot process the speed and scale of the changes we're experiencing.

///////////////////

Paradoxically, this accelerated change has forced us all to slow down and reflect on what our reality is like right now in the midst of global chaos. And what it was before Covid. And what it might be in the future.

We have the opportunity to identify what needs to change.

///////////////////

One of the dominant psycho-sociological features of the pandemic and its economic fallout has been a widespread inversion of Maslow's hierarchy of needs. Where previously many of us might have been focused on fulfilling our sense of accomplishment and even self-actualisation, suddenly we were prioritising our food supply and security needs. Suddenly our finances and careers, which we might have taken for granted before, were far more tenuous.

We all had to focus on our basic needs in response to one common goal: surviving the pandemic, both literally and figuratively (mentally, socially, financially). Together we have been forced to reassess our priorities and definitions of success, and one of the positives we can take from it is that it has proved to be a time of collective empathy. We're all in the same boat here.

From our personal problems and fragile business models to broader societal and socio-economic change, we have been challenged to confront our shortcomings as people and communities head on. As a result, we see that many of the systems and ideas that were teetering on the brink of collapse before have now been pushed over the edge.

Ground-up citizen movements have taken hold around the world, often with explosive effect. Widespread protests in the United States were the first major news events to consistently knock Covid-19 off the headlines, but they are, in fact, inextricably linked.

The pandemic has brought to the fore the tension between two concurrent trends; two sets of forces at odds with each other.

One is ultimately disintegrative and thus negative: a long-running human system that operates within a framework of fear of the unknown, segregation of the other, material accumulation for its own sake, and the relentless pursuit of individualism at the cost of the greater community.

The other is ultimately integrative and thus positive: the rapidly developing technologies, ideas, movements and discourses that aim to take humanity to its next level of development and societal integration, aligned to fairness, elimination of prejudice, and the creation of sustainable and equitable socio-economic systems.

So we see that Covid has given us, as individuals, acute insight into what is now the chronic question for collective human society. How can we do better both as individuals and for humanity as a whole?

///////////////////////

On a practical or "operational" level, sustained human progress requires us to balance our minds and hearts. These two distinctive faculties are complementary, and their partial use can lead to highly problematic actions and outcomes. For example, the overuse of heart without the balancing influence of intelligent inputs can lead to fanaticism or superstition; and the overuse of mind without the balancing influence of human heart can lead to egocentric, selfish, individualistic pursuits that culminate in negative outcomes for both the individual and the community.

Clearly, neither of these two faculties is perfect on its own. When we are no longer at the base of Maslow's hierarchy looking after our physiological and safety needs, human self-actualisation and ultimate fulfilment require new learning on how best to combine these two faculties, how to fine-tune this balance, and how to ensure that the dynamic interaction between the two never stops.

Herein also lies the global challenge now. The fact is that our human community is made up of very diverse groupings, with equally diverse blends of heart and mind. What they all have in common is the fact that their pre-Covid assumptions and predictions have been seriously challenged, and ultimately found defective.

They all have to rethink, re-imagine and reinvent their inner balance to approach the question of doing better.

In the broad answer there is another paradox: that we must now focus on individual improvement for collective wellbeing. Individual awareness, self-improvement and personal responsibility are a necessary step towards a culture that defines success and achievement in terms besides material wealth, and a system that is sustainable for collective humanity in the long term.

COMPLICATION VERSUS COMPLEXITY

To understand exactly what a new world could look like and move away from the no-man's land between past and future, we need to understand the societal shifts that Covid-19 has brought to the fore. We will delve into these later, specifically in Part III, but at a foundational level it is important to understand that we have moved from a complicated world to a complex one.

The old world was complicated, but a particular strength of our species is the ability to recognise patterns, and so we could make sense of this complicated world. We could make linear calculations according to these patterns and thus plan ahead, developing, efficient roadmaps for progress and success. We must acknowledge, in this extended conversation, huge strides in our collective welfare and quality of life that we as humans have taken in recent centuries.

Our world today, however, has become so complex that it makes reliable planning in so many aspects of life difficult, and in some areas impossible. The Covid-19 pandemic has given us undeniable insight here – the pandemic itself was not impossible to predict (there had been many warnings), but the way it would affect our globalised, unavoidably interconnected world apparently was. None of the prominent predictions in the early stages of its emergence proved to be vaguely meaningful over time, and even late in 2020, as this book was being finalised, there was little certainty about how things might go epidemiologically, economically, politically…

This is both a microcosm of the modern world and a bright-flashing indicator that we need to prepare for the unpredictable.

An obvious contributor to the complexity problem is the rapid advancement in technology, powered by the exponential growth in computing power, which we see happening before our eyes. This is a double-edged sword: a cause of unpredictability and also a potential solution to our problems.

Another contributor is the increasingly intractable generation gap, which appears to be producing two "sides" that are at odds with each other. At one end there are those born before the mid-1960s, including the Baby Boomers, who retain much of the world's wealth and power; at the other, there are those born in the 1980s and after, including Millennials and Gen-Zs, who are more technologically savvy, concerned for their collective future and demanding of change. Those born in between may be crucial in helping to forge a united path.

In a world of such complexity, of new variables and constant anomalies, all we can reliably prepare for is constant change and uncertainty. The rules of our complicated past world no longer apply, and that means we need to rewire our brains in order to start working, thinking, focusing and preparing for our new roles. We need to unlearn and relearn faster than ever before.

PART I

First, we need to focus inwards and develop the tools to strengthen our minds and hearts in the face of such tremendous and widespread upheaval. We start with eight ideas introduced in the *FutureNOW* ebook, which we have developed here for longer-term horizons. Where *FutureNOW* was about coping with the immediate shock of the acutely unfamiliar, our revised tools are intended for indefinite use into the future, to allow us to develop and deal with ongoing change with authenticity and clarity.

PART II

Next, we look at some of the reasons why society is where it is today, the stories we tell that keep us stuck in certain ways of thinking, and the ways we might awaken our imagination to tell different stories and bring about positive change. In particular, we consider the story of quantitative growth for growth's sake and the problems this creates, versus the need for qualitative growth and new definitions of success. Seeking the opportunity in the crisis, we ask how we might rearrange our socio-economic order, which prioritises long-term thinking and sustainability, to avoid a repeat of the injustices perpetuated by old stories.

PART III

Finally, we provide a real guide that offers ways of thinking about the future for consumers (that is, all of us), employees, employers, entrepreneurs, executives, policy-makers and policy advocates (again, all of us). By developing our own clear vision of the future, and identifying the path to a re-imagined future, we can start to become citizens of our abundant collective future, today.

Welcome to the FutureNEXT.

1

PART I

Embracing
the unknown

*For many of us, the disruption of the Covid
pandemic was more debilitating than the disease
itself, as it ramped up our collective fear, anxiety,
stress and depression. We need to heed the acute
lesson it has offered us, and prepare our minds
and bodies over the long term for a future in which
we handle uncertainty with ease and confidence.*

CHAPTER 1
PREPARING FOR UNCERTAINTY

As the world has evolved and technology advanced with increasing pace, so the future has become increasingly difficult to predict and plan for. Anyone who might have thought otherwise can thank Covid-19 for convincing them of this modern truth.

As a result, getting ready for the future, whether as individuals or as companies, has become less about specific scenario planning and more about building the right perspectives and having the correct fundamental approaches in place. Our challenge is to approach the future with clarity, confidence and excitement, even though it is often laced with trepidation and fear.

2020 has brought those fears about growing uncertainty to the fore. We are quite possibly the first people to witness the collapse of the world we once knew in real time, as the global pandemic accelerates us to a new age of insistent, all-encompassing change – whether we're ready for it or not.

A version of this section of the book was first released in April 2020, as an acute response to an acute need. At a time of unprecedented upheaval, the intention was to provide tools and perspective for short-term relief. Since then, we've had more time to come to terms with what has happened and adjust our mental attitudes accordingly. Now, as we start to emerge into a world shaken to its foundations, we are tasked with assessing the ideas that have grown from our prolonged collective pause for reflection, and applying them to our longer-term future.

We have a chance to emerge with a stronger, more adaptable mindset and prepare for the collective future we all want. This is our chance to escape the systems and structures that have brought us to this point; to stop chasing those ever-elusive hollow goals; to lift our heads up to the new day, and replace self-interest with the ability to lift those around us in turn.

To ensure we make the most of it, we need to make sure that we are ready to cope with the lingering anxiety, stress and fear that an uncertain future can produce. We need to prepare ourselves so we can confront the established system with a clear idea of the world we want to create, together.

With this in mind, we have identified eight fundamentals that will help gear our minds towards long-term prosperity in a world of uncertainty and unpredictability.

01 **FACE THE LOSS OF FUTURE MEMORIES**

We all paint a picture of our future in our mind.

From exciting weekend plans to our long-term career and personal aspirations, we are programmed to look forward and anchor our lives on specific goals. Whether bold or banal, we plan our way forward safe in the belief that the future will deliver us the goals we've envisioned as long as we're realistic and focused. If we're sensible, we will plan for obstacles and build in contingencies, but most of us have a pretty good idea of where we're going. In effect, we start to create memories of the future before we get there.

The Covid pandemic has had an undeniable impact on those future memories. In the short term, it cleared our calendars in 2020, utterly disrupting the celebrations, milestones and travel we had planned for the year. And in the longer term, it brought us to a stark realisation: that we cannot take our self-determined destiny for granted, as there will be times when events are entirely beyond our control. Notably, our businesses and careers have been affected in both the short and long term.

When the collective realisation of what was happening started to sink in around the globe, people everywhere began dealing with what turned out to be a hugely traumatic event. Many of us – perhaps even the bulk of us – started processing things, whether consciously or not, as the famous Kübler-Ross model of grief predicts. We worked through denial, anger, bargaining, grief and acceptance, in effect grieving for the future we'd lost and preparing to create an entirely new one. Before we could begin to adjust and start creating a better collective future, we had to mourn the lost memories that linked us to a tomorrow that no longer existed.

Longing for what may have been robs us of the energy we need to focus on our path, and the perspective we need to walk it with confidence. In contrast, mourning our future memories by working through each stage of grief is useful as it helps us make our way up the "panic barometer". We move from wondering what's happening and fearing the outcomes to a place where panic is replaced by an understanding that we now have the opportunity to create a new, possibly better future for us and others. It's the point where we swap navel-gazing self-interest for a desire to help get everyone through this, together.

As we emerge from the short-term uncertainties of the pandemic, we must be mindful that there is a longer-term loss of future memories at play. Covid has created ongoing uncertainty, and longer-term business plans and goals, in particular, may be affected. We all need to reassess our plans, and where necessary be conscious of mourning the loss of memories some distance into the future.

READ *Becoming Supernatural* by Dr Joe Dispenza for more on processing memories.

02 BECOME AWARE OF YOUR "THRIVER" CONSCIOUSNESS

The pandemic seems to have divided us into two groups: those incapable of action, and those who seem to have taken the endless uncertainty in their stride. The difference isn't intelligence or access to information – it's the maturity of their Thriver Consciousness.

The virus turned out to be a universal amplifier, dialling up our existing problems and opportunities. If you weren't enjoying your job before Covid closed down the economy, chances are you hated doing it from home. Businesses that were battling to stay afloat before were likely to fail. As reluctant couples and unfamiliar families were confined together for weeks on end, bad relationships boiled over.

Our reaction to the new world depends on the maturity of our mindset. This, in turn, is proportional to the amount of healing we've done to address the aspects of our lives that have been dragged from the subconscious to the surface by intense reflection sparked by the pandemic.

Thankfully, we can choose how to respond to this sweeping change: we get to decide if this is all happening *to* us or *for* us, by choosing to apply a naive mindset or a mature one. We can describe these two perspectives using triangles, each with different characteristics at their points, which are expansions of Stephen Karpman's Drama Triangle.

The *Naive Mindset* is made up of three negative aspects:

The Victim, where we are at the mercy of a relentless world that has robbed us of the reality we're entitled to;

The Saviour, where we convince ourselves sympathy for those suffering is sufficient, but don't take real action;

The Angry Human, where we blame everyone and anyone we can for the current state of affairs (because it displaces personal responsibility).

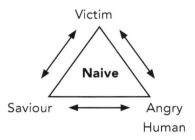

If you regularly react in this way, you're stuck in a Naive Mindset: a selfish, self-centred, self-defeating space that blinds you to your potential by forcing you to focus on immediate feelings of frustration. Don't take this as an accusation or personal attack; we are all prone to it. At any time, you may find that this mindset applies in only one or a few aspects of your life, but high-pressure circumstances – such as pandemics! – are likely to cause you to slip. No matter how much progress we make, our mindset requires constant attention and maintenance.

The *Mature Mindset* is radically different, because it helps us channel the energy we'd be wasting on misguided misconceptions and use it to become creative and positive.

It also consists of three aspects, this time positive:

The Creator, where we use our energy to actively build something new;

The Coach, where we turn sympathy into empathy and help people change their circumstances;

The Challenger, where we challenge people to do better, and help them to do so.

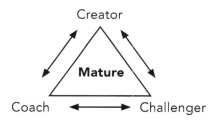

The true power of these updated Drama Triangles is as an easy-to-use development diagnostic. Take the key relationships you have with the dominant factors in your life – like money, your health and body, friendships, intimate relationships, your career and business and so on – and think about which triangle you're in with regards to each. Finding out where you have space to grow is the first step in becoming flexible and futureproof.

READ *A Game Free Life* by Stephen Karpman for more on consciousness triangles.

03 REALISE THAT
YOUR STATE IS WHO YOU ARE

How you perceive the world has a direct impact on how you prepare for it, but upgrading your perspective is not only about "getting your head in the game". It requires a daily commitment to developing the emotional, mental and physical flexibility that's at the heart of a perspective that empowers you to face the fluid future with confidence.

EMOTIONAL STATE

First, we need to recalibrate our emotional state every day.

I (John) start each day with a long meditation to address how I'm feeling, and ensure my heart and brain are synchronised. I also close my day by reflecting on my feelings to understand what I've gone through, and release whatever negativity I've had to deal with.

I also find journalling particularly useful: I focus on gratitude and identifying what could have become a worst-case scenario but didn't.

These are increasingly common rituals that have been proven to work by successful people around the world. Whatever your personal preference, it's critical that you find the right tools that work for you, and which you then use on a regular basis to maintain your emotional health and ensure you're in a position to see opportunities rather than obstacles.

MENTAL STATE

Second, we must focus on our mental state.

Try the three-directives approach. Ask yourself daily:

"What am I learning today?"

"How am I growing today?"

"When am I relaxing today?"

These questions allow you to structure your time in a meaningful pattern, and form a healthy state of mind – literally. Alternating periods of intense focus and intense relaxation improves your neuroplasticity, making it easier to learn new ideas and embrace an adaptable thought process.

PHYSICAL STATE

Lastly, ensure you look after your physical state.

I suggest two 20-minute movement sessions a day for this. You don't need to become an extremist; just respect and safeguard your body, which in turn will allow you to respect and safeguard your emotional and mental states.

This three-part combination is essential for getting into the right overall state to create the world you want rather than simply accepting the world as it is.

04 **BE CONSCIOUS ABOUT HOW YOU PROCESS THE NEWS**

For months and months, Covid-19 was everywhere. Physically, it was all over the world, but beyond that it pervaded the depths of our minds. Everyone was talking about it in every conversation. You couldn't avoid it – especially if you turned on the news. News sites, newspapers and magazines all led with Covid headlines; 24-hour television news coverage seemed exclusively devoted to the pandemic; people became obsessed with sharing statistics, graphs, graphics and dedicated "Covid dashboards".

It was overwhelming, and this obsession with the fearful, disruptive topic of the moment surely contributed to the rise in anxiety, stress and depression that have been widely documented around the world.

Immersing yourself in drama and negativity that has been packaged by professional broadcasters specifically to spike your fears and keep you engaged is the worst waste of your time and energy. It is a recipe for hysteria and personal chaos – avoid it at all costs.

Never has it been more critical for our mental and emotional states to find the balance between staying informed and inviting unwanted anxiety into our world – and as the uncertainties around the pandemic recede, we strongly advise you to bear this in mind for all news.

This is a rule that should always apply.

Limit the time you spend watching the news on a daily basis, and the time you spend discussing it with your friends and family. Try breaking it down to ten minutes for each. Any more than that can lead you down the path to the Naive Mindset, worrying about things you cannot control.

And remember, that panic and paranoia isn't limited to your television or the news sites you browse over breakfast. Social media is a shrine to sensationalism, and the virus of misinformation spreads just as quickly there as Covid-19 has in the real world. Bear in mind that false and sensational news spreads far quicker than real news (see p111), so exit groups that spread misinformation and fear, or even if they just make you feel uncomfortable. Always prioritise your emotional and mental states.

If you value staying informed, turn your attention to quality longer-form journalism, in particular weekly or monthly news magazines, where perspective can be balanced and the sensationalism of immediacy is less apparent.

Staying informed is a good strategy, but rather than panic, put your energy into creating something new.

05 **MAKE TIME DISAPPEAR**

At various stages throughout the pandemic, you may have wished that you could simply fast-forward to a time when you were "free" from the intense changes that we have all been experiencing. You can actually do this – sort of.

Rather than merely measuring the passing minutes, the trick is to make time disappear. To develop that superpower, though, we need to understand our past a little better, specifically the way that the industrial era has conditioned our thought process.

Over the years, most of us have been conditioned to take on roles that help keep the machine going – all aspects of our world, from our careers to our time, are essentially a factory of linked, linear processes that move our society forward. Even though we've evolved as technology has taken us to new levels of understanding, most of us are still taking on roles as cogs within a bigger machine. Many of us have adapted the logical, left-brained processes we've learnt on the factory floor, and used them as a framework for building lives that are methodical, sequential and linear.

However, the dynamic quantum world we're moving into will reward those who don't think that way or fit that mould. Our world is full of cogs; to differentiate yourself, you need to be something different. Individuality and authenticity are becoming more important than an ability to follow the norms – because, as the pandemic proves, the norms can change overnight.

How do we develop our most authentic, unique selves? By understanding what we're curious about and then following our curiosity.

What makes you most excited, screams for your attention when you're online or in a conversation, and sets you apart?

Exploring those interests makes you *interesting*, and that's a huge advantage in a world where there's a surplus of smart people with similar qualifications fighting for limited places in the same machine. The days of linear thinking and the same list of possible careers are being replaced by a multidimensional, new world, and we need communities of people who have embraced their invaluable individuality to avoid the same shortcomings that have always haunted our post-industrial society.

It's an outlook that will affect how you experience the day itself. When you're totally enthralled in exploring your interests, you fall into flow. You lose all track of the world around you; it's as though you've entered a wormhole that takes you from curious mind to accomplished specialist. Ultimately, it's a valuable use of time – and also a way to make time disappear.

The value of this advice is twofold. Apart from allowing you to become a time traveller, following your curiosity will also transform you into the most profitable, liberated version of yourself.

For more on the industrial revolution and how it has shaped our history and way of thinking, see p89.

06 **FORGE AN "ANTIFRAGILE" PERSPECTIVE**

Following your curiosity will not only help you find and become your most authentic self; it can also help you develop a bulletproof perspective that turns every challenge into a chance to learn and ultimately overcome. For most of us, the Covid pandemic revealed our fragilities. We struggled, in our personal lives or our business lives or both. Some, however, thrived, like the entrepreneurs who jumped at the opportunities that emerged, or the socialites who established weekly "pub nights" on Zoom. They were not fragile.

Renowned statistician and risk analyst Nassim Taleb is a strong-willed personality and not everyone's cup of tea, but his core principles are worth exploring. The book that made him famous, *Black Swan*, is about emerging from truly unforeseen events stronger than before (interestingly, he describes Covid as a "white swan" because it was not unforeseen). In the title of a subsequent book, he captured beautifully the resilience we need in the face of the events that change our reality: he says we must become "antifragile".

The concept is simple. When you drop something fragile, it shatters. But when you're "antifragile", what might have broken you before now makes you stronger. Importantly, you are equipped to deal with the unexpected.

Curiosity brings you to that state by helping reframe obstacles as opportunities to learn something new, and strengthen your inquisitive mind. Like any muscle, your ability to resist gets stronger when you exercise it, and before you know it, you'll be able to shift from shock to recovery and creativity quicker than ever before.

READ *Antifragile* by Nassim Nicholas Taleb.

07 **EMBRACE EXPONENTIAL LIVING**

Most of our lives progress in a linear, sequenced way – another lingering effect from the Industrial-era manufacturing mindset. We study to earn a degree that gets us a job where we meet our life partner who we marry while we continue to climb the corporate ladder as we raise a family as best we can before we retire and leave this world…

It's a familiar path that most of us are pushed to follow – but what happens when one or more of those stages is erased overnight?

There is an alternative to living in a linear way: living exponentially. For many of us, this is a more appropriate perspective in a new, dynamic, multifaceted, technology-fuelled world.

How does exponential living work? It starts by defining the type of life you want to achieve, and then working backwards.

A decade ago I (John) made the decision that I wanted to live a nomadic lifestyle of minimalism, bringing clarity to people around the world. That choice has helped me make decisions about everything from the people I engage with to my investment portfolio (I avoid property and lengthy contracts). Because I know where I want to end up, I can make the choices that will lead me there with confidence rather than hoping I'm taking the right next step on a path I haven't chosen.

But the impact of exponential living is deeper than that. I am more patient, because I am focused on the bigger picture and don't have a rigid timeframe to achieve things. I am calm and confident, and I can assess opportunities easily by deciding whether or not they're taking me closer to who I want to be.

The best part of this way of life is that an exponential outlook is not restricted by industry or qualification. To get started, change your "To do" list into a "To be" list. Remember, clarity comes before mastery, so commit as much time as you can to thinking about who you want to *be*, and the life you really, truly want. Write it down, then start using it to guide your choices and gather the impetus, focus and energy you need to make the life you want your new reality.

08 UNDERSTAND THAT WISDOM IS FOR THE BRAVE

This new world we are moving into is incredibly scary, because nobody has been here before. So much of what we know and understand – from education and banking to retail and relationships – has been rocked to its foundation.

The optimal way to prepare for a new future is to let go of the painful echoes from your past. It's a lesson that has become enormously relevant today in our increasingly polarised world. To initiate ground-up change that attracts support from all sides and is effective in the long run, we need to come to terms with and release any residual anger, hate and resentment we might be holding onto.

As philosopher Alan Watts observed, being wise means *un*learning something each day. Letting go of the pain and patterns of the past that restrict our perspectives allows us to walk a new and more fruitful path into the future.

Confronting pain and letting go is a painful process, one that's reserved for the brave. But even though it's uncomfortable, we all need to heal the things that hurt us in the past, so that we might take our opportunity now and into the future.

One way to gauge whether or not you have healed from your past is to spend time reflecting on people, incidents and thoughts from your past, and to determine whether or not they spark negative thoughts or emotions. If they do, then your old self remains, and you need to evolve to find the forgiveness that leads to wisdom.

Breaking the expectation of what our future should look like starts with understanding the memories that we carry with us, and deciding whether they are true or not – then deciding to keep the memories that energise us, rather than those that build resentment. In this time of great levelling and resetting, we have never been better placed to assess ourselves, our hearts and our past behaviour in an honest way, and heal what's holding us back in order to find our new selves and our new way forward.

This approach will also help us decode the dominant discourses that have created the unsustainable world we are looking to leave behind, which we cover in Part II.

READ *MAGNETiiZE* by John Sanei for more on confronting your past.

PART II

Asking new questions and re-imagining our collective future

For us to take our opportunity and re-imagine the world in a better way, we need to understand the faults and foibles that have brought about the current systemic and intractable problems. At the same time, we need to acknowledge the strides we have taken in the past and the potential we have for the future. Ultimately, we need to ask the right questions, which can shine a light on the path to collective wellbeing and prosperity – specifically HOW?

CHAPTER 2

FORGETTING THE FUTURE FAIRY TALE

What a surreal time to be alive. While we are living in a time of immense anxiety, fear and trauma, we are also living in a time of history-in-the-making; a time of incredible, meaningful opportunity. A time that demands different answers to familiar questions:

What does the future look like?
What are the trends?
Can you outline future scenarios?

Although the answers to these questions are fundamentally different, the Covid pandemic has revealed a new need: for different questions.

Across the world, hundreds of millions of people have lost their jobs and scrambled for financial relief from their governments, and are unsure of their working future. From travel to fashion, entire industries are in meltdown. Every person, business and community is feeling this uncertainty – who's to say where we'll be in a year, or five years?

The truth is that looking to the medium and long term can't offer specific reassurance right now. Attempts to do so are little more than scenario planning, which may offer insight into what *could* happen, but can't provide irrefutable, concrete answers. Expert models are notoriously inaccurate in the best of circumstances – as almost every proffered model of the pandemic spread seemed to prove – and now is not the time, we feel, to get buried in weak and conflicting data, and theories that are all riddled with built-in biases.

Rather than trying to predict the future, then, we need to understand the course we have taken and the problems that have arisen as a result – then we need to consider the future we would like to have. Do we want a future that looks anything like what we've just left behind? Should we even try to return to "normal"?

No, is the short answer – and it's a foundational principle of this book.

If we're honest with ourselves, we shouldn't want things to go back to normal. The "normal" we idealise is a mirage, a fairy tale. If it wasn't, then our previous existence, individually and collectively, would not be one that is seemingly defined by anxiety and stress – and yet that's precisely what it was. And so a "normal" future is also a fairy tale. We need to be doing things differently, both as individuals and as a collective humanity.

Inequality is a growing rather than shrinking problem. Polarising ideologies are rife across the world, with demagogues feeding off them at the most influential levels. Our women and children are not universally respected and protected. Governments and big business across the world abuse resources and power, and Covid-19 pales into insignificance when compared to the global corruption pandemic. And, of course, we continue to disrespect our environment, the precious vessel that sustains us.

This is not to belittle the idea of human progress and the general upliftment of humankind, beyond only financial wellbeing, over the centuries. Yes, we've performed medical miracles, extending life expectancy most notably since the turn of the 20th century. We have gone to the moon and back. We've raised enormous numbers of people from absolute poverty, particularly in recent decades.

There is phenomenal potential on so many levels in our tech revolution – and, at rarefied levels, there are people living astounding lives.

We will revisit these points, but that summary conveys the general point: our report card is in and we can do so much better. In this context, the most pressing question we need to answer together right now is, "What sort of collective reality do we want?"

We have an unprecedented opportunity, and even responsibility, to re-imagine ourselves and our socio-economic reality. We will rise, wiser, on a new wave of consciousness, with a sustainable mindset and humane outlook. That is our goal, and will be the destination of a challenging but thrilling journey.

It all starts with the greatest story you've never been told. Welcome to the FutureHOW.

NARRATIVES AND NORMS

To understand how to change, we need to understand how we've got to where we are today. Understanding the narratives and norms of storytelling is vital for this.

Storytelling is an essential element of the success of our species, as it allows for the transfer of information over time, and thus for our collective wisdom to grow.

As anyone who has read *Sapiens* by Yuval Noah Harari will recall, humans are wired to listen to stories, and so our lives are made up of a network of narratives.[1]

The stories we tell ourselves, listen to and believe have a profound effect on our perspective. Whether it's our favourite fairy tale or an unforgettable moment we recount again and again, stories stay with us. The problem is, stories often take on a life of their own. They grow from whisper to wisdom as they make their way from generation to generation, and before we know it, folklore and fantasy become fact. All too quickly, "Once upon a time…" becomes "We've always done it this way."

We love to hear about and hand down the traditions of those who have gone before us, sometimes with dire consequences as times change and the world evolves. Practices that we consider abhorrent today were long justified simply because generations of people accepted the stories they were told as blind truth: some people have the right to own and use other people; women shouldn't vote; children should work in labour camps or be married off; a society should be divided by a system called apartheid; and countless other historic horrors. It is a sign of our civilisation that we ultimately spot the error of these stories and start to tell new ones.

In my previous works, I (John) have written and spoken extensively about memories, and the importance of confronting and processing them. In many ways, what we remember justifies what we consider to be reasonable; for instance, a parent being abusive might justify the child's need to abuse years later. Stories also stir up nostalgic narratives as we remember how things used to be. But nostalgia is notoriously rose-tinted, so the stories of those "good times" are often embellished.

Many people are comfortable retelling ancient stories as gospel without pausing to ask whether they're true or good, and yet they will label as mad anybody suggesting that we need to make a change. This is the problem of perspective.

It reveals itself in a different way when, for instance, you're driving on the highway and you observe that the road hogs in front of you are driving dangerously slowly, while those trying to overtake you are reckless maniacs. Only you have it just right!

The point is we have conned ourselves into believing that our view and way of doing things is infallible – and that anything different should be automatically discounted. In our daily lives it means we align with people who tell similar stories, but it's a recipe for instant division, even hostility, when we encounter others. Historically it has brought about violence, brutality and the type of horrors mentioned above.

One of the richest rewards for those of us who travel extensively (before lockdown travel bans, that is) is the opportunity to see and soak up different cultures, which helps to expand our worldview and live an expanded reality that is full of possibilities. In Germany, there are parks specifically for people who prefer to go through life as naked as the day they were born. In other parts of the world, burping after a meal is a polite compliment to the chef. Try doing either of those things elsewhere, and you could end up in a fistfight – or jail.

While it may seem like these cultural differences are harmless, instinctive judgment based on what we assume to be normal automatically limits how much we can learn. By blindly accepting narratives from the past and allowing them to shape our mindset, we cut off our own ability to experiment, reflect and grow. We rob ourselves of the chance to explore, challenge our own ideas, and connect with people who hold invaluable lessons – which often take the form of stories, too. It's not an exaggeration to say that we deny what makes us human: the ability to reflect on thoughts, consult one another and evolve our perspectives.

The pandemic has done much damage, but it has also given us the chance to overhaul our old selves and move on anew; to reinvest in ourselves; and to fall in love with the ability to learn from the rich narratives of other cultures and points of view.

That is a tough ask, but it is as exciting as it is daunting. In Part I we explored the idea that wisdom is for the fearless, because it takes courage, bravery and maturity to listen and accept that everybody's view is valid to them, and thus worthy of our attention and understanding – not least because the plurality of these perspectives can add value in our own lives.

Now more than ever, we need to be open and fluid enough to listen, stretch and get comfortable with being comfortable with different views. We need to open ourselves to characters and ideas that might not fit the stories we have been told, but might expand our knowledge of the world around us.

NEW STORIES NEED NEW TERMS

To root our vision for a new future in tangible evidence, we have considered various new economies as a way to change the discourse of the digital age. We are not suggesting a communist or socialist financial system, but what might be best (though still inadequately) termed a new, humanist expression of capitalism; one that is more conscious and heartfelt because it is equally just and sustainable.

In doing so, we need to spend a cautionary moment on the broad economic terms of "capitalism", "communism" and "socialism". In much of today's polarised debate, these can be considered dog whistles that confer unhelpful and unnecessary strictures, and trigger predictable responses in their proponents and opponents.

Consider, for example, that there is a theoretical and technical equivalence between "humanist capitalism" and "sustainable socialism" or "sensible communism". And that what makes capitalism humanist are exactly the socialist elements of "socialism" or sensible elements of "communism".

In the vastly politicised and bastardised debates of the past century, these labels have suffered irreparable damage and now embody that damage.

It is hard to shed them on all sides, especially when the technical requirements of an equally just and sustainable framework/regime/ideology/ system are a set of factors – some of which are capitalist, some socialist, and some inherently and technically communist! But the protagonists of capitalism shudder at the thought of calling a humanist version something like "socialist capitalism"; rather, they avoid the fact that what capitalism is missing is a good dose of socialism to take care of the community, the collective and consideration for fairness. Conversely, there are those who would categorically "end capitalism" without thinking much beyond the full stop that finishes the sentence.

We suggest you be wary of your use and interpretation of these easy labels, and that we all look for a departure from them. Whatever our viewpoints, "capitalism", "socialism" and "communism" have all proved inadequate, unsustainable and systemically unfair in today's world. In the Covid-19 reboot moment, we have the freedom to reinvent our thought paradigm, depart from labels and rather focus on the substance, the contents and the impact. Whatever label emerges, we can live with it.

This book is a starting point of a journey of decades, but it is also the start of our search for a new paradigm. Ideologically and politically, we need to get used to the idea of "no name labels for the regimes we live in". Covid has just imposed on us a force majeure!

A case in point is the Bank of England printing cash and transferring it to the UK Treasury for direct distribution to vulnerable citizens. This is unprecedented, and is no more than a socialist act – a purer policy intervention than any socialist ideologue would have ever proposed. The US has triggered a similar intervention.

The point is this: capitalism as we know it is dead. Communism died a while back, and socialism has been in the ICU over the past few decades. And yet they all possess useful components. The challenge is to assemble them differently, shedding their historic baggage and unhelpful emotions.

CHAPTER 3

NEW STORIES START WITH NEW QUESTIONS

"When nothing is certain, anything is possible."
Margaret Drabble

Right now – and for the foreseeable future – there's no such thing as certainty.

This means there's no better time to create something new, together. As so often happens, a daunting crisis has allowed us to turn uncertainty into what would have been unimaginable. After all, even the darkness and destruction of World War II proved to be a catalyst for the new United Nations to be born – a point we'll return to.

It's in moments of collective crisis that we are forced to think big, consider every possibility, and re-evaluate the failings that saw our fairy tales and fables falter. The more fluid we are, the more exciting possibilities we'll see.

To get to a place where we can start planning our next chapter, we need to challenge the hand-me-down habits that we've normalised through narratives. But where do we begin undoing generations of fables and folklore disguised as facts? How do we pick apart the perceived truisms that have solidified in our minds as the beliefs that shape our thoughts and emotions, guide our behaviour, and ultimately define our identity?

> WE NEED TO CHANGE THE WAY
> WE ASK QUESTIONS.
> INSTEAD OF *WHY?* WE MUST START
> ASKING *HOW?*

This seems like a small shift, but it's the difference between looking back and looking forward.

Looking back and asking WHY allows us to understand the past – which has certain value at certain times, including now as we get a sense of why our past "normal" was far from ideal. But looking back also has a tendency to anchor our thinking in old stories. It inhibits imagination, encourages analysis paralysis and can steer us towards a victim mindset.

Asking HOW automatically sets our eyes on what's to come, which is absolutely critical in an uncertain future. We become creators, or at least co-creators and co-authors, of new stories and possibilities. Some of the greatest leaders in human history have understood this nuance, and used it to redefine reality.

Rather than asking, "Why is there such hatred between races?", Nelson Mandela asked, "How do we create equality for everyone?"

Rather than asking, "Why am I being suffocated by dirty energy?", Elon Musk asks, "How can we have a cleaner and better world for all?"

This was the approach that the likes of Marie Curie, Picasso, Gandhi, Martin Luther King Jr, Stephen Hawking and Jane Goodall used to change the world.

No doubt the obvious question is occurring to you: HOW can we make the shifts towards a new world?

Well, instead of asking WHY the economy is like this, we should ask HOW we can change it to benefit everyone. Rather than asking WHY we're being forced to work from home, we need to ask HOW we can find new ways of working from home that suit our lifestyle, and make sure we're working from home and not living at work. Extrapolating this – seeking the opportunity in the crisis – we can ask HOW we can re-arrange our socio-economic order to avoid a repeat of the injustices perpetuated by old stories.

Our collective challenge is to ask as many HOWs as we can, gather the answers and insights, and discover the path to the possibilities that we seek. What we need in order to find possible solutions – and ourselves – is a belief that we can create something new and that, collectively, we can write a better story.

CHAPTER 4
THE STORY
SO FAR

We have written at length so far about the need to become the authors of a better story for our species — but in order to rewrite our reality, we must get to grips with the story so far. It is a story of economics.

The harrowing loss of life caused by the pandemic has brought with it another catastrophe: the risk of widespread economic collapse. For the first time since the Great Depression of the 1930s, the world is facing an impending threat of a global depression. With hundreds of millions of jobs already lost, decades of progress in alleviating poverty in southeast Asia and the gradual efforts to stabilise volatile states could be undone.[1]

Because of our integrated financial and economic system, the very *threat* of a depression triggers fear across global and national markets – which makes that threat more likely to manifest.

These looming risks are almost too much to think about, but they should entice us to ask an important question: why is the economic impact of the pandemic, which is first a human tragedy, so prominent? The answer is simple and revealing. Money and wealth are the real root of our society's story, and that means we need to rewrite the rules that govern economics and redesign the governance of finance if we're to create a better collective reality.

DISCUSSING DOMINANCE

On the surface, the dominant narrative has suggested that the current system works: global poverty levels are the lowest they've ever been, and we have access to technology that connects us to the people and information we need to change our thinking. The average working-class family has a better life than their parents did.

If you don't look too closely, it's easy to believe that we're making progress, largely because of increased economic prosperity and ongoing growth made possible by our connected economic model. It's a seemingly simple cycle: because business has been booming, more people have money and want to spend it, which hopefully creates new business opportunities and jobs. And as this "virtuous circle" persists, so the economy grows.

While it appears that life is better for everyone, the reality is that this economic approach has grown stale in recent decades, launching a tiny minority towards exorbitant wealth, while holding the majority back. Before the current crisis, many people were demanding that we do more to address inequality. Now, the pitchforks are coming.

///////////////////////

Here are some stats about the world's dominant economy, the United States, taken from a recent TED Talk by American venture capitalist Nick Hanauer, which should make us all question the commercial love story of our before Covid-19 (BC19) world.

In 1980, the top 1% owned 8% of American wealth, while the bottom 50% owned 18%. Today, the top 1% have claimed 20% of national wealth, with the bottom half fighting for just 13%. In just four decades, the wealthy elite have become $21 trillion richer, while the bottom subset has lost $900 billion dollars (in real terms). Trapped in the centre of the struggle is the middle class, who haven't seen their income increase (relative to inflation) over the same time frame.[2]

These figures, and the growing gulf between the rich and the poor, are not unique to the US. Across the globe, the disproportionate distribution of wealth has sparked social unrest, seen the rise of fragile, false democracies and presented a platform for opportunistic, populist dictators to mobilise the masses on the back of empty promises of a living wage.

Instead of asking why the world is the way it is, we've been given a golden opportunity to ask how we've allowed ourselves to build systems that serve the wealthy – and how to do things differently.

///////////////////

Given that ours is a story of wealth and money, these financial struggles are inevitably going to bring with them socio-political challenges, which can only be overcome by developing an economic system that is no longer as focused on looking after the rich elite.

While the stories we've been told for more than a century about the resilience of certain economic regimes is unravelling, we have a chance to start seeing the truth that would have been hidden by the normalised narratives of our political leaders, defence structures, strategic security agencies and many other institutions. The pandemic has put these organisations under the spotlight, and they've been found wanting.

We can already see areas that need "fixing" – and that means we can already start asking HOW.

Our response, if we hope to create a new collective reality, must not rest on blame and consequence (although those liable must be held accountable). We need to ask HOW to fix these broken systems – because it is not smart, safe, fair or sustainable to cling to the same worldview when its shortcomings, fault lines and failures have been revealed.

PROFITS OVER PEOPLE: THE PLOT THICKENS

It's easy, and perhaps natural, to suggest that the increased success of the affluent elite is the result of compound interest, or the advantage of access to vast capital resources that allow them to assess the market and act early – but this is rarely the case. There is a massive volume of empirical evidence to suggest that it is not only "capital resources" that the elite and the successful classes enjoy; they have access to better information, social networks and points of influence, among other things.

How, then, do we allow the less-affluent similar access?

Unfortunately, governments have bought into the narratives that have given the elite access to the resources they need to maintain this system. Forced to compete in global markets, and swept up by the current of globalisation, recent decades have seen governments believe the story that they need to do everything they can to gather investment and grow, including developing policies that make their nation attractive to those seeking to protect and plump up their pocketbooks.

The relentless pursuit of growth has meant less attention has been paid to the distribution and regulation of that growth, even though our complex socio-environmental system requires growth to be sustainable, fair, shared and environmentally compatible.

There is supposed to be limited legislative involvement in a capitalist system, but the truth is that the wealthy – who influence government decision-making via campaign spending and similar instruments in many markets – are in many ways shielded from the usual array of financial threats. It's only when something like Covid-19 comes along that the vulnerabilities of the system are revealed to those right at the top.

This influence is also the reason why suggestions like increased taxes on the super-wealthy, raising the minimum wage or placing strict tax regulations on giant corporations like Amazon – who made more than $11 billion in profit in 2018 but paid no federal tax in the US[3] – are all dismissed out of hand. And it's not only a privilege reserved for mega-corporations. As the Panama Papers revealed in 2016, there are thousands upon thousands of not-so-well-known individuals and business entities engaged in similar tax evasion, often with the help of major legal and auditing firms.

Dodging taxes doesn't only affect profits, though. Weakening the tax base – that is, the number of people paying appropriate tax – makes it almost impossible for governments to look after those in need, because there simply isn't enough money in the coffers to do so. When these issues are raised and corrective measures suggested, those doing the raising and suggesting are labelled as dangerous and misguided socialists, often with dazzling mathematics, because they threaten the control of the dominant elite.

To keep feeding the economy, dominant business owners need to fuel the system. That means keeping wealth castes in place, which is partly achieved by spreading narratives that have become accepted as the natural order.

Understanding these falsehoods and fables is essential if we want to create a new reality – because most of these narratives are myths, not science.

1. "REGULATION KILLS THE ECONOMY"

The current economic narrative is that regulations constrict and ultimately kill a capitalist economy. A free market is most efficient and benefits most people when it adapts naturally to market forces. In other words, the less bothering with rules and regulations, the better – or so the story goes.

Here is a relatable story that proves the lie to this myth. In 1989 the *Exxon Valdez* ran aground in Prince William Sound, Alaska, spilling about 40 million litres of crude oil into the pristine marine parks of the area, and causing an environmental disaster unprecedented in North America and with lasting effects to this day.

The accident was caused by what are considered basic failures of maritime safety today. In the 12 years before the disaster, there had been approximately 400 separate oil spills in the Bay of Alaska, but it took the global coverage of the *Exxon Valdez* disaster to expedite the Oil Pollution Act, which was enacted in the US the following year. The Act introduced regulations such as mandatory crew rest, better navigation technology and the use of double-hulled tankers that have led to the far safer transport of oil around the world today. The number of spills has been dramatically cut, and our oceans and seas are healthier as a result.[4]

This is an incontestable real-world example of government-imposed industry regulations that should have come into effect many years earlier than they did and were widely accepted when they were finally implemented. No sane person thinks these regulations were a bad thing, and they certainly haven't killed the oil industry.

This approach applies to the broader economy, too.

As the examples of Amazon's absurd tax bill (in the US) and the Panama Papers show, without regulations that are properly enforced, billions of dollars that might be used for the public good will never materialise. Moreover, as society and technology have progressed, so our financial systems, and their interaction with our everyday lives, have become that much more complex. The lack of regulation in the subprime mortgage sector, which contributed to the 2008 financial crisis, is an obvious case in point.

Whether it's wages or competition rules, it is more important than ever to update and fine-tune regulatory frameworks to ensure the best possible outcome. And instead of relying on sweeping statements from outdated stories, we need rules that reflect the complexity of our economic environments.

The more complex the system, the more attention it needs – and the more globalised the system, the more consistent the regulatory systems need to become across the globe.

Today there is a definite and inflexible mismatch between the complexity of economic structures and the regulatory regimes in the majority of jurisdictions. In some emerging economies, the regulatory framework is on average two decades behind the changes in economy, technology and market dynamics.

This is one of those stories that need to be debunked. No market can operate without appropriate regulation. And, if they do – like the wet market in Wuhan – they can cause havoc by suddenly letting out their strain of Covid-19.

No market can operate to the benefit of a community if it's not monitored and regulated to do so. The challenge, then, is to build flexible regulatory frameworks for each market or cluster of markets, which is a more realistic approach than building one-size-fits-all frameworks, or simply having none at all.

2. "PRICE EQUATES TO VALUE"

Modern economics rests on an equation that says value equates to price. For example, a CEO who earns $25 million a year adds 1,000 times more value to the organisation than an employee who earns $25,000 a year.

This is fundamentally flawed for two reasons.

First, people don't earn what they are "worth"; they earn what they have the power to negotiate. A factory floor worker who assembles parts is a critical component of any business, and may well generate more tangible value – but the CEO signs the cheques and sits in a protected remuneration framework that the system has engineered to make sure he doesn't take his skills base elsewhere. As a result, he has significant power to dictate how much he earns. (This remuneration matrix is not necessarily created by governments; rather by the market mechanism that has evolved over the past two centuries.) Covid-19 has once again highlighted this irony in our prevailing economic and financial system; nurses, health workers and all essential-services staff are not being remunerated in proportion to the value they bring to society.

Second, there's the critical realisation that despite earning 1,000 times more, the CEO can only consume a certain amount. He can only eat one gourmet meal at a time, and wear one designer outfit, even if he owns hundreds. Wealthy CEOs cannot drive demand across the economy; they do not create 1,000 times the demand.

What really increases demand is a growing, well-paid middle and working class. They too may only be able to eat one meal at a time and wear one pair of pants, but when there are millions of them doing it, everyone prospers because there is significant demand across a spectrum of businesses of various sizes and cost points.

Then there's the tax implication of paying people better. Increasing the middle class means increasing the number of people who are able to foot the bill of social-support costs – which in turn means a growing investment in upliftment and assistance programmes. A bigger pool of taxpayers means the individual pays less, but there is more tax to help others and build a better society.

There's another simple truth here: people generate real value, and this should be reflected in the way the economy and the business enterprises that it consists of are structured. To be able to discover their own solution path, it is important that organisations aren't forced to obey the rules of one-size-fits-all thinking. They should be free to adopt a set of universal principles that promote fairness, sustainability, surplus value-sharing, and ongoing investment in research and development that ensures they are constantly delivering the most value to the largest possible community.

3. "HOMO ECONOMICUS HOLDS TRUE"

The term "Homo Economicus" means "the economic man". As economics writer Richard Wilson describes it, "Homo Economicus, or 'economic man', is the characterisation of man in some economic theories as a rational person who pursues wealth for his own self-interest. The economic man is described as one who avoids unnecessary work by using rational judgment. The assumption that all humans behave in this manner has been a fundamental premise for many economic theories."[5]

Our current economic system is not immune to this perspective; rather, it is infused by it. Businesses pursue profits relentlessly, with little or no consideration for other factors, and this focus on growth at all costs can only be built when employees – people like you and us – do the same.

Everywhere we look, we see this thinking and selfishness at play. The glamorous lives of the rich and famous are selectively sold as the dream. People are encouraged to push relationships aside in pursuit of pay cheques. We're conditioned to choose the path that leads to the highest salary – not self-actualisation and true happiness – and tend to equate the idea of being happy with the material trademarks of a luxury lifestyle.

There's a problem with this outlook, of course: a matrix of material indicators cannot be used to define non-material concepts like happiness and contentment.

One of the most destructive stories of the past two centuries is that progress, prosperity, satisfaction and social development are all measured and defined by our ability to accumulate material things. It's a tale that promotes the greed and consumerism that keeps the current system turning.

Modern economics has based its thinking on Homo Economicus, and in doing so has helped turn people into him: the selfish, greedy man who defines success by consuming and accumulating as much "stuff" as he can.

So how do we rewrite the story? The answer isn't in advocating an existence where we don't consume anything at all. Besides being unrealistic, that puts our basic needs at risk. What we need to do is elevate the rest of our complex identity.

Homo Economicus is, in fact, a human being. We are not some new species. We still have a need to care for others, to show sympathy and empathy, to understand how we can help our fellow man.

We simply do not put ourselves first all of the time. Think of the solider who jumps on a grenade to protect his unit, or the single parents who go without so that their children can eat. Think of the thousands of anonymous "Mother Teresas" around the world, volunteer and NGO workers, social and environmental activists, Doctors Without Borders, and many others who give rather than fixating on what they can gain.

Every time we act in the best interest of others rather than ourselves, we're proving this assumption of behavioural construct attributed to the modern-day economic agent to be false.

> BY ACTING IN THE INTEREST OF OTHERS, WE GIVE PURPOSE AND MEANING TO OUR LIVES, SATISFYING A DEEP NEED FOR FULFILMENT THAT GOES WELL BEYOND MATERIAL THINGS. ULTIMATELY, WE ARE ACTING IN OUR OWN INTEREST.

Reducing human behaviour to simplistic selfishness is one thing, but developing policy and economic regulations while using self-interest as a base is morally corrosive, socially destructive and wrong. It leads to the emergence of a socio-economic system that does not fit our reality.

For one, a system constructed on self-interest means that those who are willing and able to help others don't have the means to do so. As we have watched the pandemic unfold from the comfort and relative safety of our homes, we have started to appreciate and celebrate the value not only of health workers, but of everyone who supports them: the people who make and deliver their food, shelter them, and put their lives on the line for the community's benefit. Our current economic and financial universe does not recognise and reward the real value of these networks of people.

It is a tragedy that the behavioural system built to perpetuate greed has entrenched the division between rich and poor right down to the individual level, because those who are self-interested are free to pursue those interests, and those who aren't don't have the means to escape the system.

Notably, this selfish outlook is not reserved for individuals. Homo Economicus is inclined to build organisations solely to enrich shareholders, with no regard for the environmental or ethical consequences. (This is why modern corporations with individual legal identities can be plausibly described as psychopaths.) To do otherwise, they tell us, would slow economic growth and upset the equilibrium, meaning wider suffering.

Again, this is a story that no longer rings true. We're built to collaborate to seek out the best result for the group. And when we do, we thrive.

CHAPTER 5
A NEW TOMORROW

More and more academics, economists and business practitioners are starting to arrive at the conclusion that without some kind of intervention, existing economic thinking will see the pursuit of profits overpower human survival. At the very least, it will inflict untold suffering on the people caught in a volatile system that is making life worse for more and more people.

We cannot let this happen. We need to start building a new system if we hope to rewrite our reality, and that starts with understanding some important truths about people, and what we can achieve when we work together.

First, we need to realise that it's not capital that sparks true growth, but people. If we can replace our belief in self-interest and cut-throat competition with collaboration, and develop an approach that promotes reciprocity, we can unlock collective growth rather than rewarding and enriching the established elite. After all, human beings are the common denominator of all socio-economic activity. Socio-economic activity exists because we participate in and (to whatever extent) profit from being part of business and market activity. The more we're involved, the better the results for everybody.

To build a sustainable economic system, we need to include as many people as we can, and get them to work together to produce new solutions: tapping into our true nature as homo sapiens, as highly cooperative, reciprocal and intuitively moral creatures.

Then, we have to support that ecosystem by redesigning the social governance system, with all its economic, financial and technological subsystems, to promote collaboration. An eclectic network of researchers exploring economics, complexity theory, evolutionary theory, psychology, anthropology and other adjacent fields is already developing new economic models that promise real prosperity.

ENTER THE EVOLVING SYSTEM

Rather than writing a relentless story of profit, the new system tries to create a cycle that increases innovation to meet growing consumer demand. But this isn't about our appetite for advancing technology. In this instance, innovation is distilled right down to mean our ability to solve problems.

Our demand for solutions is growing, because the more progress we make, the more complex our problems become. It's a virtuous cycle in which we get better at solving problems so we can keep learning and overcoming increasingly difficult challenges. For our next evolutionary path, imagine a world of a "learning ecosystem" where individuals and institutions learn, share collective learnings and accelerate problem solving for the betterment of all.

Luckily, as the lockdown phase of the Covid-19 crisis has proven repeatedly around the world, we're programmed to work together to overcome challenges. Doctors, medical institutions and even governments started communicating in open forums without any thought of protecting or profiting from the painful lessons they had learnt. Nations readily shared equipment they no longer needed. Naval ships were converted to makeshift hospitals and NATO military jets used to transport vital medical equipment. People used their home 3D printers to produce personal protective equipment for frontline medical staff. Individuals, companies and governments in the US, UK, South Africa and elsewhere collaborated to produce simplified ventilators in a matter of weeks, a process that might have taken a year or more previously. Perhaps most prominently, the time taken to formulate and get vaccines to market was revolutionised, and research institutes and pharmaceutical companies publicly declared their intentions not to profit unduly from successful vaccines.[1]

In this environment, every element of established thinking is questioned. Competition is only useful when it pushes us to find a better solution – not to suppress other ideas. Policies need to be rewritten to help connect people, not separate classes. Instead of pursuing profit alone, we need to focus on a mix of indicators defining the business purpose.

The new approach could look something like this:

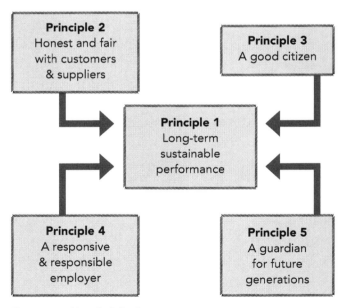

Source: www.blueprintforbusiness.org

In this new world, the difference between rich and poor is how well we find answers to our community's problems: the sum of our solutions determines how prosperous we are.

We believe that building a more sustainable, prosperous society fit for our era, driven by our collective consciousness, and engineered by our combined inputs, wisdom and aspirations, starts with five lessons, as described by Nick Hanauer in his TED Talk, that will become the defining principles of our future story. [2]

1. COLLABORATION > CAPITALISM

"Successful economies are not jungles – they're gardens," says Hanauer. They need to be tended and looked after, not left to grow wild. The market has evolved profound social technology to solve human problems, but if left unconstrained, pervasive social norms and biased regulations create systemic and even existential problems. Climate change, the crash of 2008 and the Covid-19 consequences are prime illustrations.

2. WE'RE IN THIS TOGETHER

The prevailing perspectives suggest that inclusion is a luxury that can only be considered when the elite have had their fill. But inclusion actually creates economic growth. Including more people in multiple ways sparks economic growth in a market economy. It also inspires and unleashes loyalty and creativity.

3. SERVE SOCIETY, NOT SHAREHOLDERS

The purpose of any corporation or business enterprise is not only to enrich shareholders. The new economics can and must insist that the purpose of any corporation is to improve the wellbeing and welfare of every *stake*holder, including employees, the community, the environment, shareholders and the end consumer.

4. GOODBYE GREED

"Greed is *not* good," says Hanauer. "Being rapacious doesn't make you a capitalist; it makes you a sociopath." Considering how dependent on cooperation modern economies are, it should be obvious that sociopathy is not just bad for society, but ultimately for business, too.

5. CHOOSE A NEW SYSTEM

Despite what its proponents will have you believe, our current systems is not infallible and immutable. "Unlike the laws of physics, the laws of economics are a choice," Hanauer reminds us. "If we truly want a more equitable, prosperous, sustainable economy we must have a new economics. And here's the good news: if we want a new economics, all we have to do is *choose* to have it."

CHAPTER 6
PLANTING POSSIBILITIES

Now that we've come to understand the power of HOW questions, we can take a look at the potential for change that they offer, both to each of us as individuals and to the world in general. In our context in particular, we can consider the opportunity for change that the Covid crisis has presented. Despite the widespread damage the pandemic has wrought, we may yet look back on this time in human history as a moment of clarity in our collective consciousness, a turning point for our species – or what Barack Obama might call an inflection point.

For the best chance of success, we must adopt a strong and fluid mental approach, as discussed in Part I, and frame the challenges we face in the right way. Change, for instance, can have negative or positive connotations, from the anonymous "No-one likes change" to Gandhi's "Be the change you wish to see in the world."

Of course, we must be positive. So we frame change as good, as *transformation*. Break down the word TRANS-

FOR-MATION as though it were a collection of Lego blocks, and you see possibilities begin to emerge. TRANS conveys a sense of transition, energy and change. FOR suggests movement forward as well as purpose. And MATION is just a letter away from *motion*. Reconstitute them and we have an explanation of change that is a transition with forward motion. We are moving positively into the FutureNEXT.

Using this approach, we can acknowledge the terrible and ongoing damage caused by the Covid pandemic, break it down into constituent parts and piece it back together in a way that encourages positive transformation – first within you, the individual, where all meaningful change begins, before spreading out to greater society. Covid would then become the opportunity, the accelerant, the fast track to the FutureNEXT.

Before Covid, readers could quite comfortably have dismissed such a reaction to hypothetical disaster. The changes we're discussing are a decade or more in the future, they might have argued. But now we see that major economic and societal developments have occurred all around the world almost overnight. In among the mayhem, transformative possibilities have arrived, and we have physical proof of them to refer to.

Businesses everywhere have taken a previously unimaginable leap into the digital space, affecting communications, retail, processes and, perhaps most dramatically, our workspace and practices. Once a new dynamic equilibrium is reached post-pandemic, the knock-on effects will be profound (see p131). In some ways, though, these transformations pale in comparison to the social consciousness effects that have been ignited in the digital space.

One of the hallmarks of our present-day socio-economic reality has been a widening of human consciousness. Prior to the pandemic, digital connectivity had created a shallow awareness, primarily for social and personal entertainment, but this has now been expanded into uncharted territory. We have ventured deep into the digital world for commercial operations, educational courses at universities and schools, management training programmes, and socio-political campaigning and mobilisation. Our minds have been awakened to previously unimagined possibilities.

Remarkably, we have also learnt fast, adopted with speed, and become used to doing things differently, even if it has been begrudgingly at times. The distance between "imagination" and "living the possibilities" has been shortened in an unprecedented way. This sets a relevant precedent and augurs well for re-imagining many other aspects of our personal and collective lives.

Still, though, there are many who see change as a negative; those who cleave to the comfort of the familiar, who are fearful of the uncertainty ahead. In this camp, there are those who actively search for or even promote conspiracy theories to try to make sense of things around them. (Covid-19 was caused by 5G towers, for example, or is a bio-weapon that was released intentionally.)

Luckily for me (John), I spent several months of my time in lockdown on my family farm in Magoebaskloof in Limpopo, South Africa, a place that offered stability and comfort, and came to provide a reassuring way of framing things.

Breaking things down again, farming consists of four simple stages: *preparing* the soil, selecting and *planting* the seeds, *nurturing* the fields, and *harvesting* the produce. And that's a good approximation of how we're going to create the future we want.

Right now, we are preparing the soil by unlearning outdated ideas and saying goodbye to what we were comfortable knowing. This is an exhausting process that has left many of us feeling angry, sad or even depressed, but it's crucial that we prepare ourselves for the new by letting go of the past. Extending the farming metaphor, preparing the land entails ploughing it, removing the weeds, and oxygenating the soil. Personal preparation likewise entails turning things around within ourselves, removing the unwanted and harmful while nurturing what will be required and indispensable.

And we are selecting and planting seeds by taking in radical new thoughts and ideas and applying them to our lives. This, too, can be a deeply frustrating process because of the patience and foresight required to look to the FutureNEXT while waiting for our fellow people to join us and embrace opportunity to build something radically different, and profoundly better. There is a great challenge in sensing the promise of change but not seeing it reflected in our everyday reality. Below the surface, though, new perspectives are taking root that will soon bloom into powerful new thinking. All the while we must nurture our thoughts, redefine our mental approach and guide our behaviour for best results (see Part I).

When the time is right, we must harvest the fruits of all of this change and realise the world we've been working towards – a reality where we collaborate and connect to solve problems, so that we will see more people, and eventually the whole planet, living more humane and even prosperous lives.

Right now we're doing the dirty work. We're clearing the fields, digging up the weeds and planting new ideas – preparing ourselves for new possibilities. And we're already starting to see the first signs that it's going to pay off.

CHAPTER 7
THE DEMATERIALISATION EVOLUTION

The Industrial Revolution, briefly mentioned earlier, was of such immense importance that it changed the course of human history, and its effects are still ingrained into the structures of our societies today. In 1750, according to *The Economist*, the world's richest country was about five times better off than the world's poorest. Jump back to 1500 and the difference was twofold, indicating a gentle but ongoing divergence over time.[1] Jump forward a similar period of time, to today, and the ratio is skewed dramatically, to around 180 times or more, depending on your source.[2] In between, we had the Industrial Revolution beginning in Great Britain around 1760. This is no coincidence.

This technological revolution saw the agrarian economies of the 17th and 18th centuries being systematically and irreversibly replaced by ever-expanding industrialisation, raising the tempo of production beyond imagination. Productivity increased, leading to a fall in unit costs and rapid rise in competitiveness of the industrialised nations of the West. But the Industrial Revolution did far more than just boost our ability to build stuff quickly.

As celebrated historian Niall Ferguson describes it in *Civilization: The West And The Rest*, the revolution led to six "killer apps". They were: competition, science, property, medicine, consumption and work. Collectively, these gave the West an unrivalled edge in social development and secular progress. Ever since, the West has maintained its dominance in a vast variety of developmental matrices.

Education and the sciences were transformed beyond recognition. Medicine and public health improved dramatically, and we began living longer lives as a result; average life expectancy in the UK has more than doubled from the 18th century to today (a truly remarkable fact). Industrialised nations became wealthier and their citizens more prosperous.

For these and related reasons, humankind has much to be grateful to the revolution for. Out of it came the dominance of capitalist economies, and even in recent decades we have seen billions of people, notably in Asia, uplifted from poverty as a result.

And yet it had its dark side too, the effects of which, likewise, are still with us today – and are increasingly difficult to ignore.

With the help of its six killer apps, the West managed to stage a successful, albeit costly, domination of the rest of the globe with an imperialistic mindset of raid, control and plunder. With brute force and technologically advanced hardware, European militaries secured the forces of extraction while the socio-economic ruling classes promoted secular philosophies and venerated materialism in all spheres of life. Successive theories of economic growth and social development emerged, all revolving around rising productivity, cut-throat competition between nations and the glorification of personal consumption as a primary marker of success. Rapid technological progress created a vast array of new products meeting our every conceivable need.

Meanwhile, on the socio-political front, these industrial and technological inventions brought about an ever-growing income disparity, initially between nations and subsequently within them. The relentless pursuit of growth became the norm the world over. Growth in production and in personal consumption became the hallmarks of "social development". The very definition of "development" itself took a materialistic content: it was framed in terms of income per capita, production per capita, consumption per capita, kilometres of tarred roads per capita, and so on.

During the 20th century, a two-track world emerged, one populated by hundreds of millions of people who were stuck in no-growth or low-growth regions, condemned to poverty and sub-human conditions. The other enjoyed the ostensible benefits of material progress resulting from the growth-at-all-costs model. Over time, an increasing percentage of the world population became accustomed to expecting growth for growth's sake until it, in and of itself, seemed to be the marker of success.

More!

America is the poster child for this mindset. The so-called American Dream became synonymous with a blend of materialistic growth and personal liberties expressed in conspicuous consumption. From the 1930s, its growing population enjoyed greater and greater prosperity. Business expanded, profits boomed, and for decades the US enjoyed the power of being the globe's dominant economy.

This is not to belittle American success or the positives the country has contributed to the world, of which there have been many. It does, however, raise an alarm. Growth for growth's sake simply isn't sustainable; it comes at a cost and something ultimately gives.[3]

American and Western European economic success meant that their citizens lived increasingly comfortable lives. Select other countries, such as Canada, Japan and Australia, joined the "club" of developed nations, where work and opportunity were abundant and people revelled in the certainty of sustained success.

Ultimately, though, the reality of the relentless growth approach kicked in. Rising demand on the earth's limited resources led to relatively sharp increases in commodity prices, indicating a foreseeable end to "exhaustible resources". The fear of scarcity combined with the spread of cut-throat competition between nations in pursuit of growth sparked the need for innovative production techniques. The emerging concerns about scarcity were then soon replaced with another fear: keeping the ever-expanding, entitled communities (or markets) satisfied.

The wider effects were even more profound.

The rest of the world was watching and aspiring to reach the living standards set by these chart-topping nations. But given their backlog, their growth rates had to be even higher than the developed nations' they were looking to emulate if they had any hope of reaching a comparative living standard. In the 1970s the most populous regions, Southeast Asia and China, embarked on a determined and systematic pursuit of growth to transform their nations from a state of "underdevelopment". The results have been astonishing, with hundreds of millions uplifted out of poverty in the decades since at a pace outstripping optimistic United Nations goals.

The industrialisation of China, in particular, has been astonishing – but so has the environmental devastation that has accompanied it. And as far as they have come, the likes of China, India, Indonesia and the Philippines – with a combined population of more than 3.1 billion people – have a long way to go to reach GDP-per-capita parity.

Meanwhile, developed nations have had to maintain their focus on meeting their citizens' expectations at great cost in resources and environmental effects.[4]

The fixation on growing wealth and material accumulation has come at a cost, of course, because serving a voracious and growing community requires ever more resources. For so long it was a process committed to unthinkingly by governments and their citizens without a care for the consequences.

A scene from Season 2 of the acclaimed TV show *Mad Men* illustrates the attitude well. Don Draper, the New York ad-man whose career reflects much of the accumulative, superficial wealth of the 1950 and '60s, takes his family for a picnic in a beautiful park, a local Eden. They have a happy, even idyllic, time, and then when it's time to go, Don tosses his beer can into the bushes and his wife Betty simply flicks all their picnic litter onto the grass as she packs up. They walk away without a care in the world for the trash they've left behind, but not before the kids' hands are inspected: Don wouldn't want them dirtying his shiny new Cadillac Coupe DeVille.

Back then, few people cared much for consequences beyond their narrow personal horizons, and the environment wasn't worth a second thought. The post-war economic boom was so focused on providing prosperous and material living for the world's recovering communities that the environment, inevitably, in retrospect, was neglected. In time, unsustainable environmental destruction and accelerated climate change became a reality, and their systemic impact across the globe manifested in numerous ways.

Today, we are far more conscious of the human impact on the world around us, both as individuals and governments, and yet there is still no global binding treaty to coordinate actions to mitigate the effects of climate change. (See p163.)

Moreover, we have the dilemma of developing nations to consider. While the citizens and governments of countries that have made the jump to developed-world prosperity now find themselves in a position to weigh up the ethics and long-term ramifications of how they make use of the Earth's resources, poorer populations don't have this luxury. Many in the West now see footage of smog-filled Asian cities or read about the phenomenal and growing number of coal power plants in China, India and South Africa, and despair.

Thus we see a fundamental challenge of the idea of global environmental reform: how can we do it in a way that is fair to the great swathes of people still waiting to be uplifted? How do we raise them up while polluting, literally and figuratively, less? Because up to a certain income bracket, no-one cares about the greater damage of their actions; they're just looking to cover the basics of Maslow's hierarchy – their biological survival.

There was a time when this concern was more pressing and applied in the developed world itself. The growing demand for everything from home appliances and cars to the energy and fuel that create and power them saw growing demand face off against dwindling, finite resources. By the end of the 1970s, many economists and scholars predicted that America, and by extension all the developed nations and possibly the whole of humankind, would face an apocalyptic shortage of water, food and the materials needed to maintain a prosperous way of life.

Fifty years later, though, that scenario has been eliminated from mainstream scenario-planning (though localised shortages do happen) – and herein lies the likely answer to sustainably uplifting the developing world. It's also a reason to look to the future with optimism and confidence.

///////////////////

Humanity has stayed ahead of the resources problem as a result of technological breakthroughs, and most specifically a phenomenon known as dematerialisation.

Dematerialisation is, by Google definition, "the absolute or relative reduction in the quantity of materials required to serve economic functions in society". MIT scientist Andrew McAfee is more evocative: in a brilliant TEDx Talk, he describes it as "humanity's best-kept secret".[5]

In short, dematerialisation is the point at which a community can consume more while using fewer resources. It sounds like an impossible paradox, but it's happening right now. Not only that; it's happening on a global scale. While the world population's standard of living is on a general upward trajectory – the effects of Covid-19 notwithstanding – our demand for water, energy, minerals and a number of other natural resources is actually shrinking.

How is this possible?

Due to a combination of technological innovations and incredible efficiencies.

Consider people in the street in, say, 1990 carrying portable telephones, fax machines, laptops, modems, cameras, camcorders, Walkmans (each with a thousand tapes), calculators, alarm clocks, newspapers and libraries of books with them. They would need large trolleys. Thirty years later, they need smartphones. And their phones can do so much more.

Not only is there a saving in all the material required to manufacture the dozen or so devices we no longer need, but there are all the knock-on savings in manufacturing and transport requirements. Thanks to efficient manufacturing, the phone also costs the end consumer less, and because the company can focus on one product rather than juggling the manufacturing and marketing of various different appliances, its profit margin is bigger. At the same time, more people around the world can enjoy the benefits of growing services, raising their quality of life without an adverse effect on resource availability.

The smartphone is an example of a brand-new technological device that has revolutionised the world. But across all sectors and industries, the general trend is towards not just technological advancement and digitalisation, but also more targeted and effective outcomes. In agriculture, for example, the development of "precision farming" has resulted in the greatly reduced use of water, fertiliser and pesticide per yield of crop. Farmers are using less to provide more, and the results are more consistent. The potential environmental benefits of this approach are, understandably, immense.

In the health sector, the mega-trend is towards "precision medicine" and ultimately "precision health" services. The upshot, eventually, will be far more effective, more widely accessible and cheaper medical care. Given the state of existing national health systems around the world, this approach could be a game-changer, making healthcare more affordable and socially equitable. At the same time, the data-driven paradigm lends itself to an effective division of "self-care" versus "third-party care".

Similarly, in the education sector, including training and skills augmentation, the innovations currently at play should enable the emergence of a far more widely accessible and lifelong education and training paradigm. Where is the dematerialisation at play here?

Well, in a digital age more gauged to online teaching – the move to which Covid has massively accelerated – the number of cars, buses and trains needed to transport the world's hundreds of millions of pupils and students has the potential to drop exponentially, along with the fuel needed to power them. What's more, the millions of textbooks we would have needed in the past can now be "manufactured" and "transported" digitally.

These changes should eventually trickle down to public sector organisations. Historically, the private sector leads the way in innovation while the public sector plays catchup. E-governance, for example, has a long way to go, but those who have submitted a passport renewal application from home for a country that has an effective e-service, then received the real thing by courier a few days later, will understand its potential.

Given that approximately a half to two-thirds of all nations' GDPs are used by the public sector, a wider, effective uptake of dematerialisation is essential. When it happens, the social and communal effects will be considerable, especially for the poorer and less-privileged.

From a social and communal welfare perspective, the full impact of dematerialisation will be realised when governments at local and national as well as global levels transform their modus operandi to employ technology to achieve precision planning, precision monitoring of public-service delivery, cost-effective management and accountable transparent operations. Savings and efficiency gains achieved will then translate to a more rapid upliftment of the poor without using more resources.[6]

The amazing thing about dematerialisation is that it is happening all around us, with technology helping us solve bigger problems more elegantly and with fewer resources.

An aluminium can that weighed 80 grams in 1960 now weighs 13 grams.[7]

A developing nation that is making the leap into modern-day telecommunications no longer requires the mining, refining and laying of thousands of kilometres of copper wire alongside the felling and refining of tens of thousands of trees to build the necessary infrastructure.

Cars are manufactured with less metal, so they are lighter and consume less fuel. In fact, the entire transport industry has been overhauled in a way that is imperceptible to almost anyone who hasn't thought about it in some detail: modern computer efficiencies and unit trackers allow us to move so much more with fewer aeroplanes, cargo ships, containers, trains, trucks... Just think of the model and algorithms behind Uber and Lyft to get a sense of the new efficiencies involved.[8]

Beyond the limited examples here, dematerialisation is now extending to the services sectors, financial sector, corporate services and security services – it's all around us. People can get what they want and need for less and less, and with a shrinking environmental impact.

///////////////////////

Much of the dematerialisation we have seen in recent decades has come about due to the natural power of the free market. An aluminium can with less aluminium in it costs less to manufacture. More efficient engines on machines cost less to run.

Now, Covid-19 has brought us to the brink of the first dematerialisation evolution – when, having been forced to do more with less, we have been sparked into consciously thinking about our consumption, welfare and prosperity.

Initially, as we saw in the introduction, the pandemic triggered a return to the lower rungs of Maslow's hierarchy of needs for many of us, as we focused on our wellbeing and survival rather than the pursuit of self-actualisation or worrying about our self-esteem. And we've all been asking the same question, be it as business owners or in our personal lives: how are we going to survive all this change?

This basic yet profound question takes into account a large array of interrelated changes and re-ordering, re-organisation and reprioritisation that spans personal, commercial and societal spheres of modern life. Significantly, unless these alterations and fine-tunings are made in a coherent and systemic manner, the globally interconnected and interdependent socio-economic life is bound to run into dysfunctionalities of one kind or another. On the altar of the Covid crisis, a number of changes and numerous discourses have, therefore, already begun.

Already, these shifts have forced many companies to experiment with new ways of working, and to try to forge new creative partnerships as they try frantically to reinvent themselves. Bringing together different industries and sectors with evolving challenges is a potent cocktail for the creation of disruptive, tech-heavy business ideas that need fewer resources to take off.

To embrace every opportunity in this new environment, we must understand what the age of digital abundance looks like to consumers, employees, employers, entrepreneurs, executives and policy-makers, at all levels of society. And that's exactly what FutureNEXT is about: developing new perspectives that will help us prepare ourselves and plant the seeds of possibility today to ensure we harvest and grow a profound new reality for tomorrow. In the process, we will undergo the essential transformation that leads to an era of sustainable, coherent and equitable prosperity.

PART III

FutureNEXT:
What can we do?

*It's one thing to realise that we have an opportunity
for meaningful societal change at hand – but what
can we actually do about it? Here is our advice
to you, whether you are a consumer, employee,
employer, entrepreneur, executive, policy-maker
or policy advocate.*

CHAPTER 8
THE C

What we can do:
AS CONSUMERS

When we break down global society into its smallest unit, we end up with consumers. Regardless of where we fit into the world, we are all consumers. You, the person next to you, the two of us writing this book. We are society's smallest building blocks.

How strong are these individual building blocks?

What capacity do they have to form a larger, more cohesive whole?

These are key questions in the FutureNEXT, as the unthinking consumption of our past gives way to a collective awareness of how we might do things better and more sustainably. We live in an age that allows us to better understand where our goods come from and our reasons for wanting them, and that confers on us the

108

responsibility and power to ensure that businesses serve us and our greater communities better. This ground-up awareness has been driven by the process of globalisation in recent decades and was dramatically accelerated by the introduction of online communication – and in particular by the rise of social media.

Much has been written and said about the challenges and unknowables of social media as its reach and influence has expanded across the globe since the early 2000s. One thing is for sure: it is an undeniable factor in making today's average citizen the most powerful in modern human history. Social media gives anyone with a smartphone a microphone to amplify and share their experiences, and in its relatively short life it has demonstrated its material impact on private, corporate, commercial and governmental spheres of life.

Consider the mass movements sparked and driven by social media.

In the early 2010s, the Arab Spring saw protests that began in Tunisia spread across North Africa and the Middle East, leading to major uprisings in at least five other nations, and street demonstrations in dozens of others. It provided a first meaningful insight into the mass mobilisation effects of social media, which were so central to the organisation of the protests that several governments moved to shut them down.

With origins dating back to MySpace in 2006, the #MeToo movement became another major social media phenomenon when it re-emerged with dramatic global effect in 2017. It gave victims of sexual abuse and sexual harassment a platform to reveal their personal stories, and put immense pressure on large corporations, and the entertainment industry in particular, to implement change in the workplace that was long overdue.

The following year, teenage activist Greta Thunberg came to prominence and gave real impetus to climate-change awareness by activating an entire generation of children across the world to stand up and draw attention to its impact. Social media drove the initial publicity around her, before mainstream media and high-profile personalities and politicians became involved.

And in 2020, the year of the Covid-19 pandemic that has catalysed the FutureNEXT, we have seen the resurgence of the Black Lives Matter movement to once again illustrate the power of social media. Fed up with the way the world was working, people have united and used their individual voices to generate a collective cry of rage and revolution against systemic injustice, driving change from the bottom up.

These instances all illustrate the potential raw power that we now have as connected consumers. But that power is nowhere near as effective as it might be without our learning how to harness it intelligently and use it responsibly and in good faith. Social media, for instance, is especially effective at triggering our most destructive human emotions: fear, insecurity, narcissism, anger and hatred. It is also a gateway to disinformation and conspiracy theories. A 2018 MIT study, for instance, showed that false news spreads six times faster than true news on Twitter, and untrue news stories are 70% more likely to be retweeted than true ones.[1]

Consider, now, how all the movements mentioned above ultimately developed.

The Arab Spring, sadly, did not see a broad emergence of democracy and civil liberties in the region. Instead, it saw the emergence of catastrophic civil wars in Syria, Libya and Yemen. And the moral worthiness and good intentions of #MeToo, climate change awareness and the Black Lives Matter movement were all subsequently taken advantage of by extreme elements often working in bad faith and to their own agendas. In the latter case, it quickly escalated into ongoing public violence in the US. In all examples, the perversion of the causes by bad actors has, counterproductively, come to serve as justification for those acting in similar bad faith to oppose real and meaningful change.

Perhaps there is an inevitability that social movements of such magnitude, which threaten established interests, should generate significant backlash and unintended consequences. This should, however, not undermine the positive potential of social media or, indeed, the real positive change it has already helped bring about with far less controversy. Countless good causes have benefited from their advocacy and amplification online, from crowd-funding projects and all manner of charity fundraising to higher-profile movements and the work of people who are less encumbered by political retaliation. Examples of the latter include numerous ocean clean-up projects and the female education activism of Malala Yousafzai, whose story parallels that of Greta Thunberg in some ways.

The lesson here is a timeless one: with power comes responsibility. And so we as individuals, with our recently acquired ground-up power, must learn what it means to be genuinely responsible consumers. On social media we must understand how best to maximise the benefits of, and avoid the pitfalls inherent in, the different platforms; in particular, grassroots activists need to cultivate strategies that effectively erode the power of establishments before threatening their existence. In general we must, for best effect, educate ourselves and orient ourselves in mature and meaningful ways.

/////////////////////

In an ironic turn of events, the very engines of social media, Google and Facebook, have come under severe scrutiny recently. Since 2019, US Congress has held hearings into their (and Apple's and Amazon's) monopolistic behaviours, abuse of customers' personal data, and systematic tax evasion and aggressive tax structuring.

Coinciding with further hearings in 2020, public pressure rose to the point that major multinationals, including Coca-Cola, Disney, Unilever and Procter & Gamble, felt compelled to join a boycott of Facebook advertising because of its practice of "profiting from hate". Facebook has long argued that it was merely a platform for content rather than an actual publisher, a disingenuous position that has allowed it to repeatedly evade responsibility for all the nasty material it hosts. Those protesting provided a powerful counter-argument: not only was Facebook avoiding its moral duty, but it was in the company's interest to actively promote hateful material because this attracted more user "engagement" and thus more advertising revenue. An example of the potential consequences of this approach can be seen in the targeting of US voters on social media by foreign-influence operations before national elections.

Meanwhile, both Facebook and Twitter have bowed to pressure to sanction the most powerful person in the world, the President of the United States, for some of his more untruthful and potentially harmful posts.

Within these examples, we see two profound points. One is the need for all of us, as consumers, to stay informed and responsible for our actions. Now that our voices are more powerful than they have ever been, we must educate ourselves against conscious and unconscious attempts to influence our behaviour in ways that are detrimental to society. What we choose to share and where we spend our money has an immediate and profound effect on those in our extended networks and on organisations that expect our passive consumption.

More generally, these stories highlight a fundamental transformation in the structure of power. As digitalisation and our access to real-time information is increasingly entrenched across the globe, the centre of power is shifting from institutions to individuals. Governments, corporations, military establishments and even religious institutions find themselves under the sleepless and vigilant eyes of concerned individuals, whether consumers, citizens or special-interest groups. This offers a welcome and much-needed rebalancing of the structure of power within society.

With this evolving shift of power comes the need for the assumption of responsibility, maturity and education – you might call it a growing individual consciousness. Human consciousness has never been as world-embracing as it is in our current generation, and it is safe to suggest that this is just the beginning. With every passing year, more and more evidence emerges to document our ever-expanding consciousness.

In response, there is also evidence of growing pushback from old establishments whose ideologies and commercial interests are now at risk. The rise or re-emergence of populist politics, demagoguery and blind nationalism from the Americas to Europe, of tribalism in Africa, of reactionary religious flare-ups in India and the Middle East, of global anti-immigrant sentiments, of climate-change denialism, of extreme positions being taken against multilateralism and globalisation – these are some of the divisive forces that counter the positive momentum of our time. And they are all signs that the path ahead will be challenging.

///////////////////

So we see that our time is marked by two concurrent sets of forces and trends. One is essentially integrative, made up of the technologies, ideas, movements and discourses that aim to take humanity to its next level of inner personal development and societal integration motivated by fairness, the elimination of prejudice and the creation of a socio-economic state that is conducive to sustainability and equitability. The other is essentially disintegrative, fuelled by fear of the unknown, segregation of the other, material accumulation above all else, and a relentless pursuit of individualism rather than self-awareness.

Within this paradigm of opposing forces of our time, each one of us has a choice to make, mindful of the impact that such choices have on the trajectory of social evolution, on our own welfare and on our collective wellbeing.

IN THIS CONTEXT, CONSCIENTIOUS CONSUMERS HAVE MASSIVE AND BINDING POWER. WE HAVE THE POWER TO CHANGE BUSINESS PRACTICES AND TOPPLE THOSE WHO DO NOT SHARE THE EVOLVING VALUES OF OUR GLOBAL COMMUNITY.

Our consumption choices and our voices are two critical tools for promoting fair business practices, and both have influence on all the segments to follow in this section: employees, employers, entrepreneurs, executives and policy-makers.

Now is the time to step back and realise that consumption for consumption's sake is pointless and often harmful for the world around us. Cheap goods, for instance, do not mean good goods. Often they represent production that takes advantage of people and precious resources. Cheapness can be the result of unfair subsidisation or unsustainable trade practices that lead to local job losses and the destruction of local businesses and capabilities. It can also be a driver of environmental degradation, including the pollution of rivers, oceans and forests.

This shift comes back to the doctrine of growth that we have addressed throughout this book. More mature, mindful consumers have realised that fairness and sustainability are increasingly non-negotiable, and are driving that belief with their wallets, in stark contrast to those who believe that their lives can be bettered at the expense of others.

The reality, however, is that consumer activism is a process much like all other social reforms. Not all consumers are as aware or as able to embark on activism. More often than not, poorer communities are less able to exercise choice in their consumption and have less voice. The tyranny of poverty is precisely its ability to rob human beings of choice which, as we touched on in Part I, is what happens in societies still making their way up Maslow's hierarchy. As such, those of us who have the privilege of exercising choice have an added responsibility.

A fairer FutureNEXT depends on each of us taking a stand as individual consumers, accepting the responsibility to educate and inform ourselves, and using both our social voices and spending power to support ethical and sustainable business, and starve those businesses that don't align with our values.

We encourage anyone who accepts this responsibility – and we hope all our readers do – to incorporate a system of personal awareness into your life, so that you understand yourself, your motivations and how to contribute positively to the greater societal family. This is, essentially, a call to meaningful, everyday activism as demonstrated in the choices you make on a daily basis and the way you use your voice. What it's not is the armchair activism of those who might like to appear to be proactive and civic-minded by making lots of noise on social media (frequently being "outraged") without any follow-through. Rather, it's an activism that requires ongoing mental and emotional "pre-work", as outlined in Part I, followed by real-world changes in behaviour, however small.

Note that activism can be engaged in because you *do* want something to happen or you *don't* want something to happen. Our suggestion is to fight for what you *do* want as much as possible, not for what you don't want.

ASK YOURSELF THESE KEY QUESTIONS:

- Am I self-aware as a consumer?
- What are my values as a consumer?
- Where do I spend my money?
- Why do I spend my money?
- Do I need so many things in my life?
- How might I change my spending habits for the better?
- How do I exercise my consumer activism thoughtfully and responsibly?

WHAT CAN YOU DO?

- Actively develop self-awareness and personal development skills. Read (see p188), listen to podcasts, take courses online or in person, see a coach or mentor.
- Find ways to consciously practise self-awareness, whether it's using ideas and techniques from Part I of this book or anywhere else you prefer.
- Create a group or groups on your social networks to discuss and encourage real consumer activism.
- Actively engage with your regular food and consumables suppliers. Make a conscious move to those with sustainable and ethical-practice values that align with your values.

CHAPTER 9
THE 4 Es

What we can do:
AS EMPLOYEES

For generations, people aspired to find a steady job and gradually build a career. Where they worked was not all that important, as long as the company enabled them to provide for their families. Security was key; a cool culture and shared values weren't much more than a nice-to-have.

Over the past few decades, we've seen that mentality shifting, particularly in more mature or privileged markets. While people in survival mode will take whatever work they can find, those who are a level or two higher up on Maslow's hierarchy are increasingly choosing where to work based on company culture and the opportunity to make a real difference. In turn, the value of employees in these markets is not taken for granted as it once was. There is a real drive to look after them better based on a simple corporate rationale: happy employees are less likely to leave, and are more productive and ultimately more valuable.

The FutureNEXT is going to accelerate this process dramatically, driving ever more employees into the position of prioritising business culture and purpose over loyalty and career certainty, and opening up ever more choices to those who now feel as though they work only for a pay cheque.

We will get to entrepreneurs, in the generally expected definition of the word, in a few pages' time, but even employees in traditional corporations are beginning to get to grips with the value and need for "forced entrepreneurship". In this sense, entrepreneurship is not restricted to brave souls building their own businesses; on a broader level, entrepreneurs are really just people who find solutions to problems. As more and more problems arise in our increasingly complex and evolving world, entrepreneurs are becoming increasingly vital components in all businesses.

So, while companies will be ever more motivated to provide a positive work culture for their employees, they will be equally motivated to find employees who are "task entrepreneurs", actively seeking out the most passionate problem-solvers who demonstrate plenty of initiative. This has important implications for those of us who are more comfortable in compartmentalised roles and prefer to steer clear of experimenting with new ideas.

A critical skills set for future employability, then, is entrepreneurial spirit and know-how, and one consequence of this will be the widespread temptation for more people to start working for themselves. As workers develop the curiosity, courage and practical tools of an entrepreneur, they will be attracted to the all-round flexibility that it offers in its original definition; being your own boss has obvious appeals for personal freedom and time management. Another major driver will be the technical ability to respond quickly when gaps in the market open up, unlike entrenched organisations that are famously slow to adapt. Employees who have actively developed entrepreneurial skills within their job will then be in a position to take the leap into business ownership – or personal side hustle – earlier in their careers than before.

The corollary is that nimble, adaptable yet robust organisations that choose to manage and motivate their entrepreneurial employees will be the businesses that thrive. At the same time, we are likely to see the further prioritisation of flattened organisational networks rather than hierarchies, where teams are created and connected rapidly based on need, availability and shared values.

Added to this is the undeniable fact that the advancing technologies of artificial intelligence, robotics and data science will make an increasing number of roles redundant. If the cycles of past technological advancements repeat then new roles and jobs are likely to emerge.[1] Either way, we are heading towards an intersection of the zero-margin-cost reality and the surplus society – where everyday necessities such as power, transport and data are much cheaper (approaching zero), but there are countless people with the same skills set as one another.

As we move further into the current phase of uncertainty, where change constantly appears on the horizon and companies are not as prosperous as they once were, it's not the time to predict which sector will boom or which degree you will need to stay relevant; that is to misunderstand the requirements of personal success in this new era. We cannot be asking the world to dictate what kind of values and skills we should be bringing. Rather, we should be asking ourselves what values and skills excite us, and how best to turn them into global, tech-led businesses.

//////////////////////

The Covid-19 pandemic has illustrated how old processes and economic foundations simply don't work the way they used to because they rest on levels of certainty that no longer exist. Now is the time to understand this and to change.

A KEY ELEMENT OF SUCCESSFUL CHANGE IS ENSURING THE CONSISTENCY OF YOUR INNER PERSONAL VALUES WITH YOUR OUTER OCCUPATIONAL ENGAGEMENTS AND PERFORMANCE.

The original Industrial Revolution became notorious for entrenching a disconnect between the two; for creating an army of workers who mindlessly repeated the same monotonous tasks day in day out, and in so doing lost their creativity and vitality – their "soul". The individual worker became merely another tool of production along the automated mechanical value chain for the capitalist classes, his unit of worth directly comparable with that of a spinning jenny or a steam engine. One spinning jenny might equal eight workers, for instance – a soulless equation.

The establishment of the working classes – the proletariat in the Marxian [2] lexicon – has had world-changing human and socio-political consequences ever since the 19th century. One profound impact was this dehumanisation of the worker, the separation of a person's inner values and aspirations from the outer opportunities and realities in the workplace. Today the effects are felt globally in a battle that is defining our polarising times – that between "capitalism" and "socialism" or "communism" (see box on p54).

The dematerialisation evolution currently under way offers a way out of this Manichean divide – both the internal-external divide we all face as individuals and the global divide between capitalism and socialism/communism. The solution lies in the creation of workplace opportunities that enable the individual worker to harmonise inner values and ambitions with outer possibilities. This, of course, places the onus of responsibility on the individual to become more self-aware, to actively explore his or her own capabilities, and to embark on the process of unlocking personal talents.

Which is a reminder: it's up to us to get stuck in and transform ourselves.

This mindset shift is essential for transforming the workplace into a space of creativity, opportunity and solution-seeking – a space that allows us to unlock our human capabilities for problem-solving, personal development and welfare, and self-fulfilment. By doing so, we would be contributing to the creation of a world in which there is consistency between serving ourselves and simultaneously serving broader society in as complete a manner as possible.

In our uncertain world, there are challenges ahead for all employees. Those challenges will, however, be fewer – and easier to meet – for those who embrace an entrepreneurial approach and look for opportunities to solve problems close to their hearts.

It's difficult to cast off the familiar linear trajectory of a decades-long career as we used to know it, but it *is* possible, and it is necessary. If you do it incrementally and elegantly, and gravitate towards other people in the world who are interested in the same challenges as you, you can carve out new value and make a real impact on this new world in which we find ourselves.

ASK YOURSELF THESE KEY QUESTIONS:

- Am I self-aware as an employee?
- Am I working for a company that has ethical values that align with mine?
- How am I switching on my courage to adapt and thrive?
- How do I deal with my doubts about myself and my capabilities?
- What passions do I have that can help me solve problems in my work environment and in the greater world?
- How am I switching on my entrepreneurial drive, focus and perspective?
- Am I in touch with the global shifts in my area of expertise? Am I tracking them constantly?
- Have I defined the micro-entrepreneurial tasks in my workplace and identified the ones I can take ownership of?
- Are there societal problems I can help solve?
- Can I do this within my organisation, or do I need to move outside of that system?

WHAT CAN YOU DO?

- Actively develop the skills sets related to your work. Read, listen to podcasts, take courses online or in person, see a coach or a mentor with knowledge of your line of work.
- Consider the people you can partner with – within and outside of your workplace – to make a difference at work and in broader society.

What we can do:
AS EMPLOYERS

During the Covid-19 pandemic, many employers have had to answer what seems on the surface to be an impossible question: how can we keep paying salaries while we're not generating income? Even those enterprises that were in a better position to weather the storm cannot deny that the business game has changed materially – for some businesses forever.

All affected business – which means the majority of businesses everywhere – have found themselves having to become more agile and fluid. In effect, they've been forced to think like start-ups, which contend every day with the balancing act of rising expenses versus minimal revenue. And one particular area where start-ups lead the way in innovation is a sphere of life most affected by Covid-19's acceleration into the future: our collective work spaces. Modern start-ups tend to hire staff who are self-motivated, who seek autonomy and who are naturally open to change and thus flexible working environments.

With so many people bound by law to work from home for extended periods in 2020, the incremental shift to more flexible working conditions that we've been witnessing in recent decades has taken a previously unimaginable leap in a matter of months. Suddenly, we've all seen what's possible, and corporate structuring and organisational design will be greatly affected as the world resets itself.

Technology is, of course, a huge driver here. Necessity has forced everyone, including the more reluctant older generations from which most senior management is drawn, to adapt or close down. And we've discovered – to the surprise of some more than others – that important meetings *can* be held on Zoom or Microsoft Teams, and that junior employees *can* be as (or more) productive at home as at work under the beady eye of their managers. But there is more to this than just realising the potential of teleconferencing and virtual collaboration tools.

Not only has technology enabled a complete redesign of the workplace; the public health crisis has also presented us with the opportunity to rethink the strategic purpose of the firm, its operational model and its overall impact. Corporations and mid-size companies must now reassess their over-utilisation of physical office space and the mass commuting this generates, with its associated environmental impact and the astronomical number of man-hours it costs society on a daily basis.

Some major multinationals are already making their intentions known. In August 2020, for example, the oil giant BP announced it would be selling its headquarters on St James's Square in central London, and quitting the space within two years as part of its efforts to scale back on office space. BP employs 6,500 people in the UK. Early surveys on the effects of remote working during lockdowns seemed to suggest that the bulk of companies would at least be considering a move to "more flexible working arrangements".

Even a small reduction in commuting – say, one or two days per week per individual, spread across the week – could have numerous upsides. There would be cost savings to the company in the reduction of rent and overheads; cost savings to staff in the reduction of commuting fees; time saved for staff, both on "home days" and on "office days" because of reduced commutes due to less traffic; and environmental benefits with fewer vehicles on the road.

Revised operational models will likely lead to a requirement for different skills mixes, and thus the close scrutiny of human resources. And so all indications are that the employment market post-Covid is likely to be vastly different, with successful employers having to present a different offering to attract and retain the best talent.

One trend that is likely to take off in more and more industries is the forming of distributed teams:

high-calibre teams made up of the very best people from all over the world. If the best is what a company is after, then it helps if you don't have to limit your potential employment pool to people living within an hour or two of your office. Of course, there will need to be a committed investment into the necessary tech tools and logistics to make it work effectively, but this should be easily compensated for by a reduction in central office space and overheads.

It's difficult to overestimate the importance of this shift. While it is true that many organisations succeed because of who their leaders are and how they can translate ideas into solutions, one of the most important variables in our success is who we choose to work with. Covid has provided the mass realisation that those people could be in different places and even different time zones. But therein lies the next challenge: while many companies can now effectively find employees anywhere in the world, they're now also competing against other companies anywhere in the world who have reached the same conclusion.

How, then, do you attract the most successful, creative, entrepreneurial people to work with you?

The answer lies in the previous section. As employers, we need to create an environment that is attractive to people who are passionate about solving the same problems we're taking on. Rather than investing in a few "big thinkers" and surrounding them with yes-men to do their bidding, many businesses will do better to create connected communities of problem-solvers linked, in a flatter hierarchy, by genuine passion for the broader business purpose.

Different industries are of course subject to vastly different dynamics and production practicalities. Some, such as IT, have been at the forefront of this shift for years. Others, like manufacturing, will always need central offices and factories. What seems undeniable is the hugely accelerated pace of change across the board, and we are seeing some sectors, such as the health and education services, in the throes of tectonic transformation. Both the private and public service providers of these industries operate on unsustainable and somewhat antiquated operational models.

Whatever its rate, changes are bound to transform nearly all businesses and organisations in the FutureNEXT, and employers will need to respond to their specific industry dynamics and company conditions. One thing's for sure: these developments will drastically alter the skills mix of the labour force, and with that the nature of employee-employer relationships.

Above all, being an employer in this new world is about building sustainable, fair business practices. That means treating employees fairly, starting by making them feel safe, secure and creative – which just so happen to be the perfect conditions for finding answers to the complex problems your business may be trying to solve.

Employers should look to follow the approach we introduced on p80 to underscore any organisational restructuring and the treatment of staff, complying with at least the five principles described:

1. Long-term sustainable performance;
2. Honest and fair treatment of customers and suppliers;
3. Good citizenship;
4. Being a responsive and responsible employer; and
5. Prioritising guardianship of future generations.

Putting these principles into practice will transform the nature of a business from being driven only by shareholders' interests to one that takes all stakeholders into account. Which, in the long run, will be better for the shareholders too.

ASK YOURSELF THESE KEY QUESTIONS:

- Am I self-aware as an employer?
- What is my mission as an employer?
- What impact am I having in the world?
- How much is my world changing? How often will I need to adapt, adjust and change to keep my mission on track?
- What benchmarks do I use to assess the skills mix of my team? How can I improve them?
- How often do I self-assess the treatment of all stakeholders involved in the business, including staff?

WHAT CAN YOU DO?

- Write out the impact you are making on the world as an employer, and the impact you would *like* to make. List the type of people/ employees you will need to make it happen.
- Assess the skills mix of your team at least annually.
- Work to restructure your business according to the five principles of stakeholder responsiveness on the previous page.

What we can do:
AS ENTREPRENEURS

At last, being an entrepreneur is a blessing. It wasn't always this way.

For far too long being entrepreneurial wasn't all that great, an approach to business reserved mostly for the brave or foolish. It meant going it alone against established industrial giants, and few had the fight and energy to succeed in an environment where the odds were so heavily stacked against them.

Being a self-starter even a couple of decades ago meant going against the grain from day one. After all, the current school system was developed (in the 19th century!) to build the skills needed to become employees in a limited number of industrialising companies, and society was structured to keep people safe within those steady occupations. Resisting that path made you an anomaly, even a pariah.

One country that has proved an exception to this rule was the United States, which incorporated its entrepreneurial spirit into its very identity and then leveraged it to assume global economic dominance in the 20th century. Elsewhere around the world, this approach was often seen as unnatural, too risky or even vulgar in a way, but the willingness to "fail to succeed" has become more acceptable.

Now, if you're an entrepreneur, your time has come. Welcome to an age, and world, that's been built for you. This era requires the intrinsic mindset you already have: to be uncomfortable with the norm; to be seeking solutions constantly; to cultivate the drive, energy and confidence to bring about something new.

There's a deeper sense to this, too. The world doesn't just need entrepreneurs; it needs the right kind of entrepreneurs who will find inventive ways to overcome the societal and structural challenges we face. Think of the likes of Boyan Slat, who started his quest to solve the problem of ocean plastic pollution as a teenager. Or Elon Musk, whose entrepreneurial approach envisions the complete removal of petrol-driven cars from our roads. As more information and evidence emerge, it is becoming clear that we need more than a few globally renowned entrepreneurs like Slat and Musk at work; we need hundreds of thousands of little-known yet inspiring and enterprising human beings who have the vision to solve local problems within their communities.

This is not to say that entrepreneurship has suddenly become easy. It has become more acceptable and there is more opportunity for it, but it remains a tricky endeavour, and one that requires an active approach.[3]

For starters, where are you trying to be an entrepreneur?

From a broader, systemic perspective, entrepreneurial success is heavily dependent on a favourable regulatory environment. Half a century of empirical evidence shows that societies that are successful in promoting entrepreneurship commonly have in place the following:

- Effective protection of property rights, especially protection for intellectual property rights;
- Favourable access to venture capital funding, which in turn requires supportive tax regimes;
- An effective education and training system to ensure that all the required skills are available, preferably at globally competitive costs;
- A public policy supportive of research and development;
- A socio-economic culture celebrating entrepreneurial success without frowning on failures.

Business environments that see the promotion of social freedom, transparency and institutionalised support for entrepreneurship provide a much better chance of success than those with bureaucratic hurdles, widespread nepotism and domineering state control. This may be common sense, but it's worth regularly evaluating and advocating for these conditions – or moving to them, if needs be.

Think of it this way: in commercial terms, entrepreneurs tend to disrupt the financial interests of some or other established groups, and when these groups or entities are supported by the state power it is difficult for the entrepreneurs to succeed. In many developing countries, key industries are dominated by the state; as such, entrepreneurs who hope to disrupt these industries face a David-versus-Goliath battle.

In this context, we have witnessed a somewhat facile politico-economic discourse raging globally in this field in recent decades. Almost all countries claim to want to promote entrepreneurship and inspire their youth in particular to become more entrepreneurial, and yet very few countries have managed to succeed simply because they have failed to align their commercial reality with the above-mentioned principles.

Happily, the rapid technological advances that have come to the fore during the Covid pandemic, combined with the globalisation of market opportunities, are changing these constraints, driving the process from below. The individual Davids are becoming more and more powerful. And with this growing power and relevance comes an important warning: if countries don't move fast and align their policies, there is every chance that they will lose their best and brightest entrepreneurs to other nations.

Nowadays, entrepreneurs are far more footloose than before!

////////////////////

The next question: how do modern entrepreneurs build fair, long-term, transparent solutions?

The answer comes from understanding two things: a new measurement of success, and the changing market demands.

Entrepreneurs need to understand the behaviour that is at the beating heart of this book. All over the world, there is a growing trend to define and measure success less by meeting quarterly revenue targets and more by a combination of impact and sustainable profitability – a change that reflects the emerging consciousness of the new consumer. People are coming to the realisation that conspicuous consumption and material gains in and of themselves do little more than feed our egos. We are looking for a higher purpose and developing more mature, more elegant, needs-driven wants in the process. The dematerialisation evolution is seeing our obsession with *more* begin to fade as people start to understand their place in the complex and symbiotic dance with other humans, their various communities and the Earth itself.

Those primal shifts demand that entrepreneurs embrace a more sustainable perspective – what Simon Sinek terms "infinite thinking". When we're thinking long-term, we become more patient but no less passionate, and we develop the ability to prioritise different things: the planet, our people and responsible profit. This mental framework allows us to build businesses, and a world, that we can be proud to hand over to future generations.

So, are you mission-led, building something with far-reaching impact, bringing about solutions that scale for as many people as possible?

It's a difficult proposition.

Thankfully, you're an entrepreneur – and that means you're brave enough to go looking for the answer.

ASK YOURSELF THESE KEY QUESTIONS:
- Am I self-aware as an entrepreneur?
- Am I creating short- or long-term solutions?
- Am I mission-led, building something with far-reaching impact, bringing about solutions that scale for as many people as possible?
- Am I involving my community in my business in some way?
- Am I being transparent to my staff and my customers?
- Have I assessed the business environment for the long-term success of my venture?
- Have I assessed the medium- to long-term skills requirements of my business?
- What is distinctive about the way I treat my customers and my employees?
- Am I clear about the full environmental impact of my business?

WHAT CAN YOU DO?
- Turn the concept of "failure" to one of "learning" or even "revelation". See Chapter 2 of *FOREsight* by John Sanei for more on this.[4]
- Identify the local, regional and global market segments for your solution/product. Work out how to orient your business accordingly.

- Identify those partners who love the mission you are on, as opposed to those who are ticking boxes to earn a salary. Cultivate those relationships and let the others fall away.
- Start one small initiative in the next 30 days to actively involve community members in your business and/or benefit them.
- Start one small initiative in the next three months that mitigates against any negative environmental effects that your business may generate.

What we can do:
AS EXECUTIVES

For many young people, all that really matters to them about getting their first business card is the title. A card that declares its bearer to be in some kind of executive role is a card that confers status, importance and career clout. A recent talk at a university in Dubai was a case in point: most of the students happily admitted to aspiring to be executives leading large multinational companies.

Those ambitions are, however, increasingly at odds with the reality of the FutureNEXT.

The long-desired career dream has been to arrive at the C-suite as quickly as possible, because CEOs, COOs, CIOs and CTOs have always been the ones earning the most and enjoying the most responsibility. But they face two unavoidable and growing problems, one practical, the other ethical.

///////////////////////

First, as the value of entrepreneurs continues to rise while organisations rebuild and reinvent themselves to become as nimble and flexible as possible, so the importance of executives is starting to diminish. Like the rest of us, most executives have been educated and trained to handle specific roles and responsibilities. They are engineers, lawyers and accountants who have fine-tuned their skills by earning MBAs or gathering CPD points throughout their careers. But even the C-suite isn't protected from the effect of new technologies, and with AI approaching a point where it can make critical decisions with greater accuracy, execs will need to unlearn and relearn continuously to develop into flexible problem-solvers.

This is a significant and essential shift, but it doesn't mean that executive leaders will become irrelevant or redundant. As their status declines with the flattening of corporate hierarchies, we will think of them more as partners within our collaboration community.

///////////////////

The second problem is a more insidious one; one that has gained prominence in recent decades and that cuts to the core of the themes in this book. In a world of increasing wealth disparity and societal disconnect, executives have understandably become equated with the rarefied global elite who appear to be benefiting at the expense of the majority.

Regrettably, a large number of executives around the world have amassed massive, even obscene, fortunes.

What's more, they've often done this at the cost of a destructive trail of negative real-world consequences, both on our communities and on the environment. The widening pay gap is succinctly illustrated by a 2019 report that concluded that the pay of senior corporate executives in the US had grown nearly 100 times that of average workers over the past 40 years.[5]

For so long, executives were immune to the consequences of making decisions that better their shareholders' and personal balance sheets at the expense of the real-world impact, but the FutureNEXT will see increased public pressure for this behaviour to change. The end of disengaged, unempathetic decision-making from above is on the horizon.

Perhaps ironically, those of us who are executives will come to benefit from this shift. Without the need to remain married to an organisation and sacrifice inordinate numbers of man-hours for a life climbing the corporate ladder, we will come to own our time and acquire flexibility in what we choose to prioritise, such as spending time with our families and pursuing passions rather than corporate ranking and the material gains that come with it.

Make no mistake: executives today still have an inordinate (and unsustainable) amount of influence and earning power across most industries around the world.

But as we increasingly come together and connect as a human community, fair and sustainable choices for the good of the group will become the norm, and people will aspire to be in positions where they can provide the most help rather than extract the most material reward.

If you are an executive, we encourage you to take the opportunity that the Covid pandemic has offered us, and make this leap right now.

ASK YOURSELF THESE KEY QUESTIONS:

- Am I self-aware as an executive?
- Am I building long-term value or driving for short-term profits at all costs?
- What am I *un*learning in my business?
- Have I changed my leadership structure?
- Have I assessed the consistency between my internal values and my business decisions?
- Do I apply my internal values to my suppliers, staff and associates?

WHAT CAN YOU DO?

- Assess the consistency between your internal values and your business decisions. To do so, try a practical test along these lines:

  1. Write down your top five cherished values.
  2. Assess the past quarter's key business decisions in terms of these values.
  3. Score the assessment each quarter.
  4. Check the quarterly comparisons for the past four quarters.

  After a few quarters you will see a pattern emerging if convergence or divergence occurs.

- Schedule company workshops to discuss openly the need for coherence in personal and business decisions/value within the business in general, and teams in particular.
- Develop materials to outline company values that are then made available to suppliers, staff, associates, shareholders and stakeholders.

CHAPTER 10
THE P

What we can do:
AS POLICY-MAKERS
– AND AS POLICY ADVOCATES, POLICY
INFLUENCERS AND POLICY FOLLOWERS

This section is, as you'd imagine, aimed at policy-makers. But it's also aimed at policy advocates, influencers and followers – which, as we've suggested already, is now everyone else. For those of us not in a formal seat of political or governmental power, now is the time to remember the increasing power of the consumer (or "user" or "voter"). Our power as individuals to enable change is as great as it's ever been, and policy-makers are increasingly aware of and beholden to this.

It is, therefore, our responsibility to understand the importance of policy-making across all levels of society, and to advocate for policy that is more likely to bring about a fair and equitable world.

GOVERNANCE AND POLICY-MAKING

Why, it may be asked, does governance and policy-making matter?

Can we not simply empower ourselves as individuals to succeed no matter the prevailing external conditions?

There is certainly enormous value, not to mention a certain freedom, in accepting the status quo, developing your powers of self-sufficiency and overcoming the difficulties of any given landscape. Part I of this book is dedicated to the mental fitness and wellbeing we all need to strive towards for greater success in life and business, no matter the realities and uncertainties of what's going on around us. But, as we've seen, the intention is ultimately a selfless one; a process that should be oriented towards our communities and humanity as a whole. And part of that ongoing process is in bringing about change in the systems that affect us on a daily basis, which ultimately applies to the strategic policies on which our societies are built.

The reality is that business enterprises, industrial innovations, technological progress and personal initiatives all take place within a regulatory system, and require a reliable and predictable legal framework. The more complex a socio-economic system becomes, the more governance and policy-making become a binding factor of success. There is a point beyond which mental fortitude – the willpower to pull yourself up by your bootstraps – simply isn't enough.

Just ask the many restaurateurs and events coordinators around the world who had to close their businesses when government responded to the Covid pandemic with policies that prevented people from congregating in groups.

Or imagine, for instance, if the internet was made illegal where you live. What would become of businesses in your area? How would it affect your personal life? This may sound like an unlikely hypothetical, but in many countries the availability and reliability of internet is poor or intentionally restricted. Why? Because of poor governance.

The same lesson applies across so many regulatory spheres, though not always with such obviously severe consequences.

/////////////////////

The Covid crisis has made clear the importance of public policy on our personal, commercial and financial lives. What began as a public health scare soon mutated into an unprecedented challenge for public policy-making at all levels. The global economy was brought to a near standstill, and many thousands of businesses were ruined while hundreds of millions of jobs were destroyed. The consequences of the pandemic will unfold for years, and it will be a long time before we can calculate the real extent of the damage.

As we've seen, employers, employees, entrepreneurs and corporations are in the throes of unprecedented tectonic disruptions. This was an existing phenomenon, but much of the action has been brought into focus and catalysed by the Covid crisis.

As badly as we may be affected personally, governance institutions have been doubly as affected, irrespective of their ideological and historic track record. Not only have they had to govern and offer policy framework in a highly unpredictable and unsettled environment with agitated citizenry, they had to do this while their own internal organisational structures were being subject to the same dynamics.

Governance institutions are typically not the pioneers or trailblazers of innovations; they are the adopters, a lag that compounds the political and ideological strictures. This is true at all levels of policy-making – local, national, regional and international – although there are specific challenges at each one. Policy experts have been pointing out these increasingly problematic fault lines of governance over the past half-century, and the lived reality of citizens has increasingly confirmed the problems. But never before have they been as clear for all to see as in the light revealed by the Covid crisis.

///////////////////

One of the notable false dichotomies of recent history is the supposed choice to make between following the group and adhering to central leadership versus distrusting the collective and maximising self-interest.

In the first instance, we're told our leaders have all our problems under control and as citizens we shouldn't worry; they've got this, the solution will be handed down to us. In the second, we're conditioned to believe that we as individuals have to take matters into our own hands or be crushed in the maelstrom; it's us or them.

Both these philosophical paradigms have psychological appeal, and both have been revealed to be problematic and unsustainable. They are found in societies all over the world, but nowhere is the clash between them more evident than in the ongoing political polarisation in the United States, where their extremities are constantly tested by a cycle of negative reinforcement. For objective observers, of the US and elsewhere, it is clear that the reality of our communal and interdependent existence is far more complex than either group gives credit. Collaboration and nuance are vital in designing a fair and sustainable system of governance.

As we have outlined already in Part II, homo sapiens of the 21st century has become an ever more complex species, individually (our "inside world") and collectively (our "outside world").

Yet if we examine our socio-economic and political systems, we don't see a matching evolution in our key governance institutions. Our religious leaders conduct themselves, as they have done for millennia, as having superior knowledge and insights into the way the world works that their followers should accept without questioning. Our political leaders and parties still operate, largely, in the old mould of "leader-follower", with its inherent superiority-inferiority assumption. And our corporate leaders, likewise, assume the historic role of command and control – even their titles have remained "chief officers" of operations, information, finances and so on.

The point is that society has changed dramatically while governance structures and policy-making paradigms have lagged far behind. In fact, they have remained largely intact for well over a century, increasingly out of sync with the inherent requirement of the complexities of modern life. And, as we've touched on throughout the book, the signs of malfunction are everywhere to see: grinding poverty despite the positive technological developments that mean there is now plenty to go around; millions suffering from obesity and the illnesses of overeating while millions more suffer from hunger; trillions of dollars being spent on war machines while hospitals and healthcare systems are under-funded; outdated and neglected education systems no longer fit for our time; exorbitant salaries paid to executives while the working classes live hand to mouth. And these contradictions are all underscored by the twin evils of private and government corruption: corporate malfeasance and market manipulations on the one hand, and politicians extracting public resources, directly and indirectly, on the other.

THE ESSENCE OF THIS BOOK CANNOT BE MADE MUCH CLEARER THAN THIS. THINGS NEED TO CHANGE.

Intellectually we know this to be true, and now practice is following theory, with intensifying uncertainty and violent ruptures revealing themselves across various subsystems, from socio-political ruptures to financial and economic meltdowns. The real-world ramifications are there for us all to see: the violent racial and political tensions in the US; anti-immigrant movements in Europe and elsewhere; the rise of crass nationalism across the globe; the flaring of tribal and religious sentiments; and in general a swelling of hostility towards "otherness".

Whether appropriately or ironically, our newfound digital technologies have made such movements and developments widely visible to all, and have exacerbated and even caused many of these fractures. We are as connected as we have ever been as a species, and yet the profound loss of social cohesion is evident everywhere.

Governments and policy-makers, always lagging, have never been further behind. They find themselves in an unenviable position, with successful and effective models a rarity, and a revolution in governance and policy-making now at hand.

This is the revolution that our modern societies need irrespective of their ideological histories, one that is necessitated by the irreversible changes we've undergone and a redefinition of the power structures within society and in all its subsystems. A key element will be the way historic centralisation of power is replaced by a flatter hierarchy where power is more equitably dispersed to the member individuals; that is, to everyday citizens.

Within this new evolving paradigm, the FutureNEXT will see the rise of ethical, transparent and participatory leadership. When power is dispersed, the definition of leadership changes. Policy setting can no longer be unilateral or top-down, and so mechanisms will have to be found to enable policy formation that involves all stakeholders in an open and trustworthy way. On the grandest scales, that means literally everyone! (If that seems a stretch, consider the Swiss approach of holding regular referendums to guide policy-making.) At the same time, the leaders will become the "servants" of their communities, without excessive and unwarranted pay or privileges.

This, then, is the overriding mega-trend in our contemporary evolutionary social path.

In this setting, value generation, creativity and innovation reside in the masses, who have the confidence and the trust that their innovations and hard work will be respected, and their rights and entitlements protected. For those in power, and accustomed to protected positions and benefitting from unwarranted privileges, this may be hard to accept. As such, alongside this mega-trend there will be a visible pushback by many established institutions vested in the "old world order".

//////////////////////

Fallout from the Covid pandemic has hardened the societal stance against ineffective public policies and dysfunctional leadership without values and principles. For those in power there is simply not enough room to manoeuvre any more, and doubling down on broken and faulty systems has only helped to widen social fractures, commercial failures and human sufferings.

If we reframe the crisis, though, this becomes the perfect opportunity to consider alternative possibilities in the midst of a daunting crisis of uncertainty.

AFTER ALL, WORLD-CHANGING
POLICY OVERHAULS HAVE BROUGHT
REAL AND EFFECTIVE CHANGE
THROUGHOUT HISTORY,
AND THEY HAVE OFTEN BEEN
CATALYSED BY DISASTER.

It was during the dark and destructive days of World War II that the opportunity for the creation of a "united nations" sparked into existence. The notion of national social welfare emerged in the first half of the 20th century from the crisis of disparities of income distribution in Europe; this came on the back of unparalleled wealth generation by the industrialist classes following the technological successes of the 19th and early 20th centuries. And the birth of the modern state itself was precipitated by the social crises and political upheavals that followed the spread of the Industrial Revolution.

More than two centuries later, the world is opening up to the realisation that the modern state needs modernising, at governmental and municipal levels. To this end – and in this process – the more fluid we become, the more possibilities we will see. The FutureNEXT is, therefore, forward-looking, nimble, adaptive and informed by the errors of the past and imperatives of the present.

THE ECONOMIC SYSTEM'S FUTURENEXT

The challenge that the Covid pandemic has brought to the fore is how to effectively shift a system that prioritises the rich elite over everyone else. It is a challenge that humanity has, in fact, risen to in recent centuries, with the normalisation of human rights for all and the upliftment from poverty of billions of people – a sure sign of civilisational progress. But the trend in recent decades has seen a temporary reversal in many areas of progress.

Now our existing economic system, its associated financial subsystem and its socio-political framework are bound to test new stress levels. And this is the case for developed countries! In the emerging economies, such pressures will likely cause multiple tensions and at times social implosions of various kind.

In 2020, nearly every world government created unprecedented levels of public debt in a matter of months. This has been justified on the altar of "saving lives", but here another false dichotomy has emerged: between "saving lives" and "saving livelihoods". The result has been a worldwide lockdown of the economies, rapid contraction in economic activity and record job losses. At the time of writing, in late 2020, estimates suggest more than 400 million permanently lost jobs.[1]

Large-scale national debts were created – or exacerbated – as the underlying economies were forced to stall, and the result has been a double whammy: we've run up a huge bill but drastically reduced our ability to pay it off. It will take generations to gradually pay off this debt, and even then this will only happen if governments start building their nations' balance sheets in a multiple of the rise in debt. In effect, we need to generate new streams of revenue to enable our nations to service their ballooning public debts and to be able to pay them off over time.

One of the hot topics that emerges as both a contributor and potential solution to our current crisis is globalisation. For many of us, globalisation is an indicator of the advancement of human civilisation, the coming together of humanity as one species with a shared story, and thus a process at the heart of the sentiment in this book. One of the dominant socio-economic forces of the last century, it has accelerated in the digital age – but there has been pushback, which we see in the re-emergence of nationalistic and anti-immigration movements. Whatever your position, this is not necessarily a cut-and-dried issue. The rapid spread of Covid around the world, for instance, casts globalisation in a less familiar light.

What is certain, however, is that globalisation is a genie that has been uncorked and, though it may not always be optimally managed, it is here to stay. The world is too deeply interconnected now, via all manner of intertwined socio-economic and cross-cultural tendrils, for countries to consider themselves in isolation. There are operational inter-dependencies in almost all sectors of the global economy, and at the most fundamental geographical levels countries share, use and pollute the same atmosphere, oceans and waterways.

And so the task of rethinking the structures and systems of our governments and economies must not only be determined by national leadership, but as importantly by a coordinated global policy paradigm. Yet many political leaders and policy gurus still tend to ignore these realities and pursue and promote nationalistic policies for growth and development. Such approaches hold little, if any, prospects for sustainable growth. Even less promising are those policies that aren't just self-serving and nationalistic, but are hostile to the interests of other nations.

The FutureNEXT thus requires a mindset shift towards globally coordinated, socially fair and environmentally sustainable economic policies

THE SOCIO-POLITICAL SYSTEM'S FUTURENEXT

We have seen how our global socio-political system faced the Covid crisis with, in effect, serious "preconditions" to begin with. Systemic ruptures and potential societal implosions were to be expected. Here, again, is where our opportunity lies.

We can see with the naked eye the systemic fault lines that need fixing. The stories we have been told for more than a century about the resilience of various governance regimes are unravelling before our eyes. Democratic, authoritarian, statist, secular and religious political regimes have found themselves wanting. None has proven fit-for-purpose, none resilient enough to manage the consequences well (although some have undeniably done better than others).

Covid has vividly revealed, among many things, the vast inadequacies of the national and global security our political leaders assure us we need. Where so much human time, energy and capital is devoted to defence structures and strategic agencies, we are discovering that many threats are false or at best exaggerated while others have been overlooked at catastrophic cost. When the moment arrived, when the enemy struck in the form of an invisible (and yet predicted) virus, our strategic institutions were put to the test and found wanting.

The surest and most relevant proof of this today is in comparing global budgets allocated to military defence versus those allocated to defence against infectious diseases. For instance, a common point of comparison has been that of the annual defence budget of the United States versus its annual budget for the Centers for Disease Control: the former was $738 billion for the 2020 financial year; the latter was a little more than 1% of that. [2]

You don't have to be a pacifist to recognise that both war *and* disease are real threats to society, and that the respective budgets allocated to fighting them need close scrutiny. We would suggest that fit-for-purpose modern governments should be cooperating wherever possible to combat short-term existential threats such as pandemics, nuclear war and unknowable advances in artificial intelligence.

//////////////////////

Systemically, two glaring fault-lines have emerged, one at intra-national level, the other at international level.

The first has seen a catastrophic loss of "social capital" in many nations around the world, in different and accumulative ways. Social capital is built up over time as a society and its members grow in trust, empathy, promotion of reciprocity, and the cultivation and celebration of philanthropy. It's vital for the sustainability and reliability of collective welfare, both at the local and at the national level, because human societies require as much social capital as financial capital to function. Sustainable prosperity necessitates a healthy balance between the two.[3]

A critical cause of this loss in social capital has been the inability of governments all around the world to maintain social coherence and rally a sensible and effective response to fight the pandemic. This is not to say the task was an easy one – but the failure has been irrefutable and disastrous. Almost since the moment the outbreak started generating headlines in early 2020, public trust in national responses has been rapidly eroded.

Adding fuel to the fire, the inability of political leaders to manage the crisis in a credible and participatory way has caused a public health crisis to mutate into so many other expressions of divisive national rancour. Nations have found themselves visibly fractured, their existing public policies questioned, and the overall legitimacy of their governance institutions undermined.

The secondary knock-on effects of poor governance are fairly predictable. When unethical and incompetent people operate in governments, abuses and corrupt practices lead to the loss of tax morality and an increase in tax avoidances. This in turn reduces the pool of public funds, which then weakens the ability of the government to take care of vulnerable groups in society. This vicious cycle of "poor governance of the modern society" further destroys that critical requirement of success and prosperity, namely social capital.

A growing number of countries now find themselves in this self-destructive spiral.

Similarly, the second fault line, at an international level, has seen the operational integrity and effectiveness of global organisations come under severe strain, most prominently those that operate under the auspices of the UN and its agencies. They have been found inadequate on many different fronts – and given our pressing need to find global solutions, this is no small catastrophe.

Again, this is not a new phenomenon – experts and thought leaders have been sounding the alarm for years – yet it took the Covid crisis to highlight the potential damage that such dysfunctionalities at the global level can cause to all nations, rich and poor alike.

WHERE TO FROM HERE?

It is the definition of insanity to do the same thing over and over and expect a different result, and we have seen that if we carry on with the same modus operandi we are going to reproduce the same terrible results. It is, therefore, not intelligent, safe, fair, sustainable or sane to keep at it.

An obvious question then emerges: how do we fix the problems?

And, of course, there is no neat prepared answer. There are, however, some clear starting points.

First, we must understand that anyone with a neat prepared answer is probably selling a solution from one of the existing paradigms that have been proven, repeatedly, not to work. In so doing, they are likely protecting their own interests and little beyond. In the classic polarity we see so often nowadays, it may come in the form of a negative: capitalism/socialism hasn't worked, therefore the answer is socialism/capitalism. Real answers require understanding and nuance, commitment and effort. (See box on p54)

Second, we must take a genuinely scientific approach – that is, one that blends imagination with a good dose of idealism, checks the facts of experimentation, and assumes a smart but humble posture of learning. We must embrace the unfailing scientific loop: "action-reflection-evolutionary refinement". We must reject the rise of anti-science opinion and "subjective facts", which has become little more than a disingenuous way of protecting specific interests.

Third, we must open our minds and orient our thinking towards the HOW questions raised in Part II of this book. We have to begin to seek solutions; to raise the many HOWs; to think in different and diverse ways, unexpectedly, out of the box; to throw out the old and unproven stories (but to retain the kernels of truth they may still hold); to open both the mind *and* the heart; to consider all options and engage in the path to "solution discovery".

The two fault lines in our collective socio-political sphere outlined here are inseparable. Both intra-national and international complex issues of socio-political nature require a total rethink. Within the paradigm of the FutureNEXT, we believe the guiding principles of evolutionary, participatory, fair and sustainable governance framework are:

- Celebration of genuine diversity, including diversity of thought, within society and among nations;
- Acknowledgement of reciprocity and respect among diverse groupings;
- Acceptance of equal responsibility for collective security and prosperity;
- Respect for fairness, transparency and justice; and
- A transparent and participatory division of national authority and responsibility, versus international delegation of authority and responsibility.

ASK YOURSELF THESE KEY QUESTIONS:

- Am I self-aware as a policy-maker, or as an advocate, influencer or follower of policy-making?
- How much of my business and personal success do I attribute to favourable public policies?
- How much of my fears and doubts do I apportion to unreliable political and regulatory frameworks?
- How much am I involved in shaping appropriate and value-driven public policy changes, both locally and globally?
- How does my business participate in local and global policy formulation, advocacy or activism?
- Have I assessed how my business solutions may contribute to solving certain public policy challenges?
- Have I reviewed my policies to ensure they meet global benchmarking?
- Have I reached out to my target groups, communities and individuals to hear their response to our policies in practice?
- Have I got mechanisms in place to collect regular responses to the effectiveness of our policies?
- Have I got a reference panel to give independent feedback on the impact of our policies on business, on the environment, on job creation and on other vital areas?

WHAT CAN YOU DO?
- Identify the global policy-making concerns that affect your personal and business success; for example, those to do with the environment, human rights, immigration laws, customs controls, or gender, racial and civil equality.
- Identify and then advocate for three critical public policies that will make a difference to you and your business.

CONCLUSION

For many readers, the call for a great paradigm shift in human society may appear unfeasible or too drastic. Yet we believe this is the type of thinking that would have assumed, only a few months ago, that "doing business without premises" was unfeasible or "having a successful national or international corporation without having a sizeable team of staff under the same roof" was drastic.

Before Covid, these would have been considered insurmountable disasters. But in lockdown we had the will – and the technological means – to overcome them. Why? Because the alternative was far worse.

We need to harness this experience and this logic in our policy-making challenges today.

The astoundingly good news is that we have the technological means to provide basic human rights for everyone in the world, and to enable solutions to our existing problems. Only a few decades ago this notion could not have been entertained by economists and policy-makers.

And we now have recent experience of how we can successfully respond to disruptive and evolutionary disasters, with necessity proving the most powerful driver. What's more, we can take inspiration from the fact that, while our centralised governments have failed us, private companies, initiatives and citizens dispersed across the world came together in constructive collaboration to provide many of the success stories of the pandemic. The sequencing of the virus's genome, the medical breakthroughs in treatment and vaccine creation, the repurposing of factories and infrastructure to make PPE and medical equipment, the inspiring stories of human spirit and charity – these are glimpses of our potential that shine a light on our way forward.

As we have highlighted repeatedly in this book, we have what it takes to transform our malfunctioning institutions. We have further underscored that our individual and collective success in this new evolving world order requires a compatible and supportive governance and public-policy paradigm. And with the changing structure of power, we all, personally and collectively, have a role to play in fast-tracking the required transformation.

What we offer here is merely a beginning. We hope you rise to the challenge and join us in finding new ways forward – for ourselves as individuals and as members of the human race.

Clearly, real action is the intelligent option.

ENDNOTES & RESOURCES

FutureNEXT has been inspired by the many authors, professionals, scientists, clients, peers and teachers who the authors have interacted with over the years.

As with his previous books, John notes: "I have absorbed, adapted, borrowed and refashioned their work in an ongoing process of continuous research, from face-to-face interactions and hearing them talk in person and online, to reading company reports, blogs, articles, websites and more. For this I am hugely grateful – hopefully, I have given back to them in return."

Iraj's contributions draw from his personal learnings, published research, books and body of work that goes back decades.

In these Endnotes, the authors reference specific sources by chapter, with additional notes on the text in places. There follows a supplementary reading list that has informed the book.

Chapter 2
[1] *Sapiens: A brief history of humankind* by Yuval Noah Harari (Vintage, 2011)

Chapter 4
[1] "Hard times forecast for global job recovery in 2020, warns UN labour agency chief" (30 June 2020): news.un.org/en/story/2020/06/1067432

[2] "The dirty secret of capitalism – and a new way forward" by Nick Hanauer (TEDSummit, July 2019): www.ted.com/talks/nick_hanauer_the_dirty_secret_ of_capitalism_and_a_new_way_forward

[3] "Amazon will pay a whopping $0 in federal taxes on $11.2 billion profits" by Laura Stampler (14 February 2019): www.fortune.com/2019/02/14/ amazon-doesnt-pay-federal-taxes-2019/

[4] *50 People Who Messed Up The World* by Alexander Parker and Tim Richman (Robinson, 2017)

[5] "What is homo economicus?" by Richard Wilson (25 August 2018): www.investopedia.com/ask/ answers/08/homo-economicus.asp

Chapter 5

[1] See "AstraZeneca: won't profit from Covid-19 vaccine in pandemic" by Danica Kirka (30 July 2020): abcnews.go.com/Health/wireStory/astrazeneca-profit-covid-19-vaccine-pandemic-72080355.
This was a declared intention. As of late 2020, it remained to be seen how vaccine rollouts might play out around the world. Vaccines, unlike chronic medication, are poor profit-generators for pharmaceutical companies – will their stated good intentions in the face of public expectation hold in the longer run? Either way, the pharmaceutical industry is ripe for close scrutiny. Pharmaceutical companies, which receive vast government grants, walk a notoriously tight ethical line. They are ostensibly at the forefront of the advancement of human health and wellbeing, but they also generate enormous profits from the optimal protection and pricing of their patents and drugs. We would argue that a more just world would try harder to find ways to make more medicine more widely available.

[2] "The dirty secret of capitalism – and a new way forward" by Nick Hanauer (TEDSummit, July 2019): www.ted.com/talks/nick_hanauer_the_dirty_secret_of_capitalism_and_a_new_way_forward

Chapter 7

[1] "Economists are turning to culture to explain
wealth and poverty" (3 September 2020):
economist.com/schools-brief/2020/09/03/
economists-are-turning-to-culture-to-explain-
wealth-and-poverty

[2] The Global Finance website, for instance,
published a calculation in July 2020 that adjusted
gross domestic product (GDP) per capita relative to
purchasing power parity (PPP). The result had Qatar
at the top on $132,886 and Burundi on $727 at
position 192. See "The world's richest and poorest
countries 2020" by Luca Ventura (30 July 2020):
gfmag.com/global-data/economic-data/worlds-
richest-and-poorest-countries

[3] The problem of growth for growth's sake
is clear to see, and perhaps at its most refined,
in the attention-extraction advertising model
of modern social media, which relentlessly seeks
out user "engagement" to generate advertising
opportunities. The longer social media platforms can
retain the attention of their users, the more they can
target them with customised advertising. They do
this by employing the finest software-engineering

brains and most sophisticated AI in the world to
manipulate and deceive our fallible human brains,
triggering our worst addictive responses without
a care for the consequences along the way –
consequences that affect individuals (causing
addiction and mental-health problems, such as
increased anxiety and depression) and society as
a whole (creating extreme community polarisation
and influencing elections, among other things).
This is possible because of the wholly inadequate
regulation within the tech industry, which mirrors the
inadequate regulation in other industries (see p68),
and the misguided belief that an industry guided by
quarter-on-quarter profits can self-correct. As Justin
Rosenstein, former engineer at both Facebook and
Google explains in the Netflix documentary *The
Social Dilemma*, which unpacks this phenomenon,
"This is short-term thinking based on this religion
of profit at all costs, as if somehow magically each
corporation acting in its selfish interests is going to
produce the best result." See *The Social Dilemma*,
directed by Jeff Orlowski (Netflix, 2020).

[4] Increasingly, these costs are being extracted
from the developed world and thus assigned to their
carbon-emissions output. For example, China, India,

Indonesia and the Philippines have dramatically increased their per-capita carbon emissions in the past five decades, even as the likes of the US, UK and France have made significant inroads into theirs. But a large element of this phenomenon can be attributed to the globalisation of manufacturing; in effect, developed nations have outsourced their pollution to developing nations. According to Worldometers.info, China, in assuming the role of de facto factory for the world, increased its share of global carbon emissions from 2.54% to 29.18% between 1971 and 2016, increasing its per-capita consumption about sevenfold. In the same time, the United States's share of global emissions grew fractionally from 12.45% to 14.02%, while its per-capita consumption dropped more than 25%. Given that air is not bound by national borders – and bearing in mind the greater context of this book – this serves, first, to illustrate how important global cooperation is on the matter; and, second, to underscore how the relentless demand for consumption has become globally pervasive. Thus we see that the integrity and sustainability of our environment cannot be "nationalised" – there has to be a global regulatory framework.

[5] "Dematerialization: Humanity's biggest surprise" by Andrew McAfee (TEDxCambridge, May 2018): www.ted.com/talks/andrew_mcafee_dematerialization_humanity_s_biggest_surprise

[6] The UAE, for example, is using blockchain to enhance efficiency in government. See "Blockchain in the UAE government": u.ae/en/about-the-uae/digital-uae/blockchain-in-the-uae-government

[7] The International Aluminium Institute: packaging.world-aluminium.org/benefits/lightweight

[8] For more on dematerialisation, including the vast efficiencies improvements in transport, listen to MIT scientist Andrew McAfee talking to Sam Harris: samharris.org/podcasts/170-great-uncoupling

Chapter 8
[1] A key finding is that this phenomenon is due to human use, not as a result of bots. We are prone to spreading false news. The authors of the study suggest this may be due to the novelty of false news; that is, people like to be first with new news. They also believe this phenomenon is likely to repeat itself across other social media platforms.

Collectively, we need to learn to restrain this urge
and spread news responsibly. "Study: On Twitter,
false news travels faster than true stories" by Peter
Dizikes (8 March 2018): news.mit.edu/2018/study-
twitter-false-news-travels-faster-true-stories-0308

Chapter 9

[1] Every time a new wave of industrialisation or
technological advancement emerges, it leads to
a material change in the structure of the economy
and the associated pattern of job creation. One
mega-trend emerging from the successive
industrialisation and technological innovations is
the reduction of physical efforts needed to produce
more. Human inputs into the production process
have progressively become less brawn-intensive
and more brain- or intelligence-intensive over time.
In the decades and centuries ahead, it seems likely
that intelligence-intensity in turn will diminish, giving
way to intuition, insights and perception-intensity.
As a result, the proportions of brawn, brain and
intuition/insights in the production process will
evolve. This in turn will entail a change in the skills
profile needed for the emergent economic structure.
It is now a given that human beings' comparative
advantage is not in brawn power: we realised way

back in human history that oxen and horses, for instance, are far superior. Intelligence and insights, on the other hand, are distinctive attributes of homo sapiens, and in the journey along our evolutionary path, it seems likely our economy will reflect more and more of those distinctive human attributes. By extension, then, materialism will gradually and systematically be balanced by our need for humanity, spirituality, ethics and morality. This will be the platform for an optimal balance, or the sweet spot, to create authentic human beings, reflecting a balance between the inner quest for peace and happiness, and outer efforts to contribute to a fair and sustainable socio-economic environment.

[2] In our polarised world, it is worth noting our deliberate use of the term *Marxian* rather than *Marxist*. *Marxian* gives respect where it's due to Marx and his many valid observations, though it does so without implying any kind of thrall to him. *Marxist*, meanwhile, is now an overtly politicised term, which is in itself problematic as it eliminates any kind of nuanced discussion. And Marxist perspectives, predicated on Hegelian principles that ultimately nullify human spirit and spirituality, certainly are problematic, if not counter-factual.

[3] A fascinating and intrinsic element of entrepreneurship is the "failing" and learning process. For so long, the term "failing" has had a repugnant connotation, but for entrepreneurs "failing" is integral to the process. One reason why entrepreneurship is becoming more accepted and widespread is because we are beginning to learn that shedding the fear of failure is a real ingredient of success. More accurately, we need to learn how to learn from our failures. At the end, we realise that the journey of success has many hills and valleys, and that it is filled with bouts of successes and learnings or even revelations (as opposed to failures). If we are able to inject this attitude into our formal education system and child-rearing culture, we will be able to socialise human beings to minimise, if not eliminate, the term failure. In that kind of ecosystem, people continuously pursue their passion, talents and imaginations and, via a humble posture of learning, they can follow a journey of entrepreneurship in search of self-discovery. Ultimately, by doing so, they can bring their unique entrepreneurial input into the collective dynamics of social development, and serve the community at large.

[4] *FOREsight* by John Sanei (Mercury, 2019)

[5] The report was issued by the Economic Policy Institute, which those who dispute it might describe as left-leaning. A common counter to the idea that such a growing pay gap is an ethical problem and morally unsustainable is that it doesn't account for the value generated by executives. A second is that CEOs "are not getting paid at the expense of workers"; that if they were paid less, the money would go elsewhere. Both arguments are weak. On the first point, executives cannot generate value without complementary production factors, notably their staff. Yes, every building needs an architect, but the best architects cannot realise their vision without competent builders, and no competent builder can deliver on the proposed design without reliable and hardworking labourers. The fair recognition and rewarding of various contributions made by different role players is key. Over the past five or so decades, we have fallen into an unequitable pattern that has encouraged a widening income gap between executives and their staff. Executives are rewarded with their annual salary and bonuses along with share options and/or equity ownership, while staff/workers receive their annual salary and their bonus in the form of a 13th cheque. As a result, the execs have both short-term increases (salary and bonuses) and

long-term gains (stock option increases), while staff only receive short-term increases. This drives the income inequality gap, which will only grow until the pattern is disrupted. On the second point, it's simply not true that if executives don't receive as much remuneration, that money will go elsewhere. Every company has a pool of funds to be split between "management/staff" and "dividend going to the shareholders". If within the management/staff pool less is taken by the executives, then there will be more to split among the workers.

Chapter 10

[1] "Hard times forecast for global job recovery in 2020, warns UN labour agency chief" (30 June 2020): news.un.org/en/story/2020/06/1067432 The estimate of 400 million full-time jobs lost equates to more than 13% of the world's workforce, according to the International Labour Organization. Note that these are constantly evolving figures, and were best estimates when this book went to print.

[2] "Pentagon finally gets its 2020 budget from Congress" by Joe Gould (19 December 2019): www. defensenews.com/congress/2019/12/19/pentagon-finally-gets-its-2020-budget-from-congress;

"Coronavirus and NIH/CDC funding" by Chris
Edwards (16 March 2020): www.cato.org/blog/
coronavirus-nih/cdc-funding

[3] For more on social capital, see "Social capital:
The critical factor for developmental success" by
Iraj Abedian (June 2014): irajabedian.co.za/social-
capital-critical-factor-developmental-success

SUPPLEMENTARY READING LIST

Personal development and conquering shadows
Antifragile by Nassim Nicholas Taleb
  (Random House, 2014)
Becoming Supernatural by Dr Joe Dispenza
  (Hay House, 2017)
A Game Free Life by Stephen Karpman
  (Drama Triangle, 2014)
The Infinite Game by Simon Sinek
  (Penguin Business, 2019)
MAGNETiiZE by John Sanei (Mercury, 2018)

Global governance and reforms of the UN
"Global governance and the emergence of global
  institutions for the 21st century" by Augusto

Lopez-Claros, Arthur Dahl and Maja Groff
(23 September 2019): iefworld.org/governanceWG

"Governance in the age of virtual reality – from data
to experience" by William Hamilton (30 November
2017): globalchallenges.org/governance-in-the-age-
of-virtual-reality-from-data-to-experience

"Collective actions for global public good:
Toward self-enforcing agreements" by Howon
Jeong (30 March 2017): globalchallenges.org/
collective-actions-for-global-public-good-toward-
self-enforcing-agreements

"Who cares about global governance?" by Manjana
Milkoreit (30 September 2017): globalchallenges.org/
who-cares-about-global-governance

Social capital and communal reciprocity

"Social capital: The critical factor for developmental
success" by Iraj Abedian (9 June 2014): irajabedian.
co.za/social-capital-critical-factor-developmental-
success

Social Capital: Theory and research by Rene Dubos
(Routledge, 2017)

Sustainability and social justice

"Intergenerational equity and the political economy
of South Africa" by Iraj Abedian (24 February 2014):

irajabedian.co.za/intergenerational-equity-and-the-political-economy-of-south-africa

"Towards a just economic order: conceptual foundations and moral prerequisites" by Bahá'í International Community (29 January 2018): bic.org/statements/towards-just-economic-order-conceptual-foundations-and-moral-prerequisites

"Shared vision, shared volition: Choosing our global future together" by Bahá'í International Community (23 November 2015): bic.org/statements/shared-vision-shared-volition-choosing-our-global-future-together

"Modern societies and ethical values" by Iraj Abedian (6 November 2013): irajabedian.co.za/modern-societies-and-ethical-values-2

Human happiness and development

"Development, human happiness and the challenge of distinguishing means from ends" by Daniel Perell (5 August 2014): bic.org/perspectives/development-human-happiness-and-challenge-distinguishing-means-ends

"Can we have prosperity without growth?" by John Cassidy (10 February 2020): newyorker.com/magazine/2020/02/10/can-we-have-prosperity-without-growth

ACKNOWLEDGEMENTS

JOHN
Much gratitude to my parents for opening up their arms and welcoming me to their farm to be with them in lockdown, and growing a friendship we didn't have pre-Covid. And to the wonderful people who helped bring this all together. And to all those who have lost loved ones because of Covid, or businesses, jobs or relationships, or otherwise suffered.

IRAJ
I would like to acknowledge my family's support during the lockdown, and when I was absent and lost in the world of researching and writing of this book. Much of my inspiration was fired by Shoghi Effendi's missive on "The unfoldment of world civilization" (11 March 1936), Professor Michio Kaku's numerous works, and Professor Steven Phelps's work on "Impelling the development of consciousness". Thank you to them all.

WWW.JOHNSANEI.COM

 johnsanei

WWW.IRAJABEDIAN.CO.ZA

 IrajAbedian